RAVI ZACHARIAS & VINCE VITALE

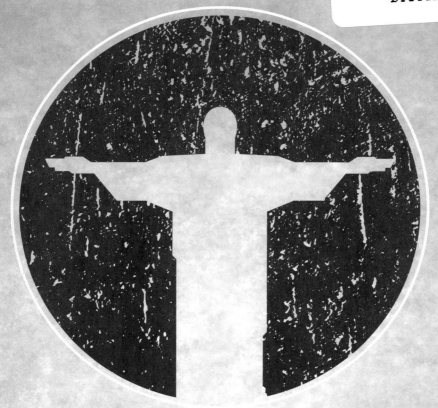

JESUS
AMONG SECULAR GODS

LIFEWAY PRESS® NASHVILLE, TENNESSEE

VINCE VITALE
Writer

**EDITORIAL TEAM
GROUPS MINISTRY PUBLISHING**

Michael Kelley
Director, Groups Ministry

Brian Daniel
Manager, Short-Term Discipleship

Joel Polk
Editorial Team Leader

Reid Patton
Content Editor

David Haney
Production Editor

Jon Rodda
Art Director

STUDENT MINISTRY PUBLISHING

Ben Trueblood
Director, Student Ministry

John Paul Basham
*Manager, Student
Ministry Publishing*

Karen Daniel
Editorial Team Leader

Stephanie Livengood
Editor

Amy Lyon
Graphic Designer

Published by LifeWay Press®.
© 2017 Ravi Zacharias and Vince Vitale
Reprinted Feb. 2018, June 2018, Nov. 2018

ISBN 978-1-4627-7757-0 • Item 005799067
Dewey decimal classification: 231
Subject headings: GOD \ JESUS CHRIST—DIVINITY \ GODS AND GODDESSES

To order additional copies of this resource, write to LifeWay Resources Customer Service; One LifeWay Plaza; Nashville, TN 37234-0113; fax 615-251-5933; call toll free 800-458-2772; order online at LifeWay.com; email orderentry@lifeway.com; or visit the LifeWay Christian Store serving you.

Printed in the United States of America

Student Ministry Publishing • LifeWay Resources
One LifeWay Plaza • Nashville, TN 37234

Table of
CONTENTS

About the
AUTHORS

RAVI ZACHARIAS is the founder and president of Ravi Zacharias International Ministries (RZIM). For forty-five years, Zacharias has spoken all over the world in many universities, such as Harvard, Dartmouth, Johns Hopkins, and Cambridge. He has addressed writers of the peace accord in South Africa and military officers at the Lenin Military Academy and the Center for Geopolitical Strategy in Moscow. At the invitation of the president of Nigeria, Zacharias addressed delegates at the first annual prayer breakfast for African leaders held in Mozambique. Zacharias has direct contact with key leaders, senators, congressmen, and governors who consult him on an ongoing basis.

Born in India in 1946, Zacharias immigrated to Canada with his family twenty years later. While he was pursuing a career in business management, his interest in theology grew; subsequently, he pursued this study during his undergraduate education. He received his master of divinity from Trinity International University in Deerfield, Illinois. Well-versed in the disciplines of comparative religions, cults, and philosophy, he held the chair of evangelism and contemporary thought at Alliance Theological Seminary for 3½ years. Zacharias has authored or edited more than twenty-five books. He and his wife, Margie, have three grown children, and they reside in Atlanta.

VINCE VITALE is the director of the Zacharias Institute. He was educated at Princeton University and the University of Oxford, and he later taught philosophy of religion as a faculty member at both of these universities. It was during his undergraduate studies in philosophy at Princeton that Vince took an unexpected journey from skeptic to evangelist. He then completed masters' and doctoral studies at Oxford.

While researching at Oxford, Vince developed a new response to the problem of evil. This response, termed the nonidentity defense, is discussed in Vince and Ravi Zacharias's book *Why Suffering? Finding Meaning and Comfort When Life Doesn't Make Sense*. In 2017 Vince and Ravi released a second coauthored book, *Jesus Among Secular Gods: The Countercultural Claims of Christ*.

Vince has commended the Christian faith at many universities, including the University of California, Berkeley; Johns Hopkins; Carnegie Mellon; Princeton; Oxford; and Cambridge. He has also spoken at Google headquarters and Passion City Church.

Vince is married to Jo, who also works with RZIM as the dean of studies for the Zacharias Institute.

INTRODUCTION

Only the truth of Jesus can answer the deepest questions of life. The popular "isms" of the day leave the most fundamental questions unanswered. But how can believers learn to respond with grace and truth to these secular gods? *Jesus Among Secular Gods* is designed to equip believers to give a reason for the hope they have (1 Pet. 3:15).

The rise of secular gods presents the most serious challenge to the absolute claims of Jesus since the founding of Christianity itself. Not only has the Christian worldview been devalued and dismissed by modern culture, but its believers are also openly ridiculed as irrelevant. In this study, Ravi Zacharias and Vince Vitale challenge the popular "isms" of the day, skillfully point out the errors in their claims and providing convincing evidence for the absolute truth found in Jesus.

This study will prepare you to face today's biggest challenges to the Christian faith head-on. It will help seekers understand Jesus' claims and will provide Christians with the knowledge to express why they believe Jesus stands tall above other gods.

As you complete this study, you will not only learn why Christianity stands tall above secular gods, but you will also be prepared to explain the claims of Christ with gentleness and respect to a world that has embraced these "isms" with fervor.

ACKNOWLEDGMENTS

Many people worked diligently to make this project possible, and we are deeply grateful to each of them. Randy Pistor showed enormous skill, insight, and generosity in his work on the Personal Studies for this project. With her characteristic distinction, Danielle DuRant offered meticulous and discerning comments during the editing phase. My trusted agent, Andrew Wolgemuth, was an eminently wise and attentive guide through the entire publication process. The commitment to excellence of Joel Polk and the entire LifeWay team pointed at every turn and in such an encouraging way to the ultimate excellence of Jesus, who is both the inspiration and the aim of this project.

How to
USE

Jesus Among Secular Gods provides a guided process for individuals and small groups to explore major secular worldviews and examine how followers of Jesus should respond to them. This Bible study book includes six weeks of content, each divided into two main sections: "Group Time" and "On Your Own."

GROUP TIME

Regardless of the day of the week your group meets, each week of content begins with the group session. This group session is designed to last one hour, with approximately 20 minutes of teaching and 40 minutes of personal interaction.

Each group study uses the following format to facilitate simple yet meaningful interaction among group members, with God's Word, and with the video teaching.

START
This section includes questions to get the conversation started and a review of the previous week's study.

THIS WEEK'S TOPIC
This section introduces the content for the current week.

WATCH
This page includes a place for students to take notes as they watch the video. It also identifies key terms and definitions referenced in the session.

DEBRIEF
This section includes discussion questions and statements that guide the group to respond to the video teaching and to relevant Bible passages.

ON YOUR OWN

BRINGING UP YOUR FAITH
Here students will find the week's question and a few thoughts to help them begin conversations with people who are not yet Christians.

JOURNAL
A journal page provides space for students to reflect and process the conversations they have each week with non-believers.

PERSONAL STUDY
Two personal studies are provided each week to take students deeper into the ideas that shape secular worldviews and to guide believers to respond to these ideas from a Christian perspective. These pages challenge students to grow in their understanding of God's Word and to make practical applications to their lives.

ADDITIONAL RESOURCE

Consider going even deeper into this content by reading the book on which this Bible study is based: *Jesus Among Secular Gods* (FaithWords, 2017), ISBN 978-1-4555-6915-1.

Be Prepared

START

Today, we have all sorts of information at our fingertips but we have no idea how to answer the most fundamental and important questions of life. We live in a time filled with choices, with an endless menu of beliefs on our digital doorstep; an age of offense, when choosing one belief over another labels us as narrow, exclusive, intolerant, and extremists; and an age of distraction, when social media takes up hours of our days. These three factors make it more difficult than ever to make an informed decision about the deepest questions of life.

What are some of the biggest questions people ask about life?

One of those big questions is: *What is the meaning of life*? Take a few minutes to record a one sentence answer to this question. Then, share your answer with the group.

How do your answers differ? How are they alike?

What a gift it is that Jesus gives us so many ways to respond to that central question of life! When faced with these big questions, we can become absolutely paralyzed as we choose how to respond. This is why the Bible tells us we should always be prepared to give an answer for what we believe.

In your hearts revere Christ as Lord. Always be prepared to give an answer to everyone who asks you to give the reason for the hope that you have. But do this with gentleness and respect.
1 PETER 3:15

THIS WEEK'S TOPIC

This is one of the most difficult times to be a Christian. When it comes to the Christian faith, the cultural landscape has shifted, and the challenges have intensified.

It used to be that if you were a Christian, people thought you were a little weird, maybe even naive. Today, Christians are often targeted as the enemies of progress. Now more than ever, we need to be prepared to defend a Christian way of seeing the world. But can faith be defended?

Richard Dawkins wrote:

> *Faith is the great cop-out, the great excuse to evade
> the need to think and evaluate evidence. Faith is
> belief in spite of, even perhaps because of, the lack
> of evidence.*[1]

The biblical definition of *faith,* on the other hand, comes from Hebrews 11:1:

> *Now faith is the substance of things hoped for,
> the evidence of things not seen.*
> **HEBREWS 11:1, KJV**

Which of these two quotes do you think accurately describes faith? Why?

Blaise Pascal—the brilliant seventeenth-century mathematician, physicist, and inventor turned theologian—claimed that God has given us enough evidence to believe in Him rationally but not so much evidence that we can believe in Him based on reason alone.

Do you think that is a fair statement? Why or why not?

What rational reasons do you have for believing in God? What elements of your faith go beyond reason?

WATCH

Use this space to take notes as you watch the video for Week 1.

1. Christianity doesn't ask us to be _____-____-_____.

2. The _____ of Christ is central to the apologist.

3. Sometimes _____ come en route to faith.

4. Sometimes God _____us in different situations in our lives, but ultimately takes us back to why He is the _____.

5. Receive all questions as a _____.

6. Sooner or later, if you don't _____ the question, _____ _____ will.

7. The day you stop asking questions, you are either fallaciously assuming you are _____ in your knowledge, or you've really _____ growing.

8. If you do not answer the _____, you really aren't answering the question.

9. _____ has become such an assumption in our time.

10. Everybody has a _____.

WORDS TO KNOW

Absolutes: a principle that applies to all people, whether they choose to believe it or not; unrestrained or without exception

Apologetics: the argument or justification for your beliefs; why you believe what you believe

Existential: from the heart; relates to our experience of existence

Philosophical: from the head; relating to the pursuit of wisdom; basic values, beliefs, ideas, and attitudes of an individual or group of people

Secularism: belief system in which one is either indifferent to or rejects religion

Answers: 1. know-it-alls; 2. lordship; 3. questions; 4. meets, truth; 5. gift 6. ask, somebody else; 7. infinite, stopped; 8. questioner; 9. Secularism; 10. worldview.

DEBRIEF

First Peter 3:15 says:

> *In your hearts revere Christ as Lord. Always be*
> *prepared to give an answer to everyone who asks*
> *you to give the reason for the hope that you have.*
> *But do this with gentleness and respect.*
> **1 PETER 3:15**

What are the five instructions given in this verse? Highlight the one you find most challenging.

When people ask tough questions about God and no one takes their questions seriously or provides them with good answers, they often conclude that good answers to their questions must not exist.

What is a question about faith you've been afraid to ask because you thought people would not respond well?

Have you ever asked a question about faith and felt that you were looked down on for doing so? Share about that experience.

The health of the church in the days ahead will mostly be determined by the way we handle questions.

How can we help make the church a place where challenging questions about faith are welcomed and affirmed?

What are two or three questions about faith you hope you are never asked by a non-Christian because you would not know how to answer them?

If you knew the questions in advance for an interview for your dream job, you would spend time preparing to respond well to those questions. The opportunity to remove an obstacle to faith in a person's life is even more important than getting your dream job, so you need to take the time to be prepared.

What can believers do to be personally prepared to respond to questions about faith?

What is one way you hope to be better equipped as a result of this study?

PRAYER

- Read Ephesians 3:14-21, and make Paul's prayer your own. Ask God to do immeasurably more than all you ask or imagine, according to His power that is at work within you.

BRINGING UP YOUR FAITH

Use the following questions to start a conversation with a non-believer this week.

Make it a goal this week to ask the following questions of someone who is not yet a Christian.

> **What is your biggest objection to Christianity?**
> **What do you think it would take for you to change**
> **your mind about God and become a Christian?**

Remember that, when we defend and share the faith, we want to win the person, not just an argument. God didn't come to save questioners with clever answers; He came to save questioners through a relationship with Him that is founded on grace. We need to model grace, and that begins by being good questioners and good listeners. Remember:

> *Behind a question is a questioner, and if*
> *you do not answer the questioner,*
> *you are really not answering the question.*
> **RAVI ZACHARIAS**

All questions should be received as gifts. The answer to every legitimate question is something true, and all truth is grounded in God. Therefore, every question, even the most hostile, is an opportunity to share something about who God is and what He has done.

For Christians, asking tough questions is not a sign of a lack of faith but an act of worship. When you think about it, asking questions and listening well to the answers is the way you get to know a person. The same is true of God. God is not a theory—He is personal. Therefore, asking deep questions about Him is the way you get to know Him better.

As you have conversations about faith, remember that listening to the response is as important as asking the question. Listen attentively and sympathetically to the answers you receive. Be ready to respond to their questions, even if you do not have all the answers.

JOURNAL

Use this page to reflect on your conversation.

Whom did you talk with? What was your overall experience with this conversation?

How willing was the person to have a conversation with you? What obstacles did you encounter?

What insights did you gain about communicating truth with gentleness and respect?

FAITH AND REASON: IS FAITH BLIND?

Imagine you overhear someone say, "I've been doing some reading, and while Jesus may have been a decent moral teacher, He certainly wasn't God. All that stuff about His death and resurrection was made up centuries later by corrupt church leaders who were after power and money. It's all legend; there's nothing historical about it. That's why they call it faith." Then another person asks you, "Is he right? Is Jesus' resurrection just a legend?"

How would you respond?

THE MEANING OF FAITH

Take a moment to think about the word *faith*. How would you define it?

Compare your definition with the following two definitions.

Faith, being belief that isn't based on evidence,
is the principal vice of any religion.[2]
RICHARD DAWKINS

Faith is a response to evidence,
not a rejoicing in the absence of evidence.[3]
JOHN LENNOX

How does your definition compare with these two definitions? To which definition is yours most similar?

In what important ways do these definitions differ in their understanding of the relationship between faith and evidence?

Which definition do you often see used by the world and by the church?

THE CONNECTION BETWEEN FAITH AND EVIDENCE

While it may be surprising, even to some believers, Lennox's definition is actually the true biblical definition of *faith.* The Bible explicitly defines what *faith* means: "Faith is the substance of things hoped for, the evidence of things not seen" (Heb. 11:1, KJV).

Rather than translate the Greek word *elenchos* as *evidence,* newer translations use *assurance* or *conviction.* As a result, the connection between faith and evidence is sometimes overlooked. However, the connection becomes even stronger when we consider that *faith* is a translation of the Greek word *pistis,* which includes the idea of trust.

Putting these pieces together, we see that biblical faith is ultimately belief and active trust in God, based on the spiritual perception of the evidence He has provided us. In other words, biblical faith is anything but blind! To quote Lennox once more, "Just as in science, faith, reason, and evidence belong together."[4]

The next time you're engaged in conversation and someone says, "Belief in God is just blind faith," how could you respond?

LOVING GOD WITH YOUR MIND

In Romans 12:2 the apostle Paul wrote, "Do not conform to the pattern of this world, but be transformed by the renewing of your _____."

Without looking up this verse, what word would you expect to fill in the blank?

Now, look up Romans 12:2 in your Bible. What did Paul tell us to renew? Does this surprise you? Why or why not?

Nurturing the mind is incredibly important for the Christian faith. In fact, it is one way we worship God. When Jesus was asked about the greatest commandment in the law, He replied:

Love the Lord your God with all your heart and with all your soul and with all your mind and with all your strength.

MARK 12:30

This comes from a key verse in the law, which commanded the Israelites to:

Love the LORD your God with all your heart and with all your soul and with all your strength.

DEUTERONOMY 6:5

A visual comparison of these verses reveals something interesting.

Deuteronomy 6:5	Mark 12:30
Heart	Heart
Soul	Soul
Strength	Strength
	Mind

As you reflect on this, consider why Jesus added the mind to the list of ways we can worship God. *(Hint: Read 1 Cor. 2:12-16.)*

It seems natural to say, "Love God with your heart," because the heart—the seat of our will, desire, and emotions—is frequently connected with love in our culture. It also seems natural to say, "Love God with your soul," because the soul is the very essence of our being. But practically speaking, loving God with the mind may be less familiar.

Read each of the following verses in your Bible. Record how each verse provides us with a way to love God with our minds.

- **Proverbs 1:5**

- **Proverbs 9:9**

- **Proverbs 10:14**

On a scale of 1 to 10, 1 being not at all and 10 being all the time, how well are you loving God with your mind? Mark a number on the scale.

How does loving God with our minds prepare us to give a reason for our Christian faith?

What is one step you will take to love God with your mind this week?

A REASONED DEFENSE

RECLAIMING ARGUMENT

The word *argument* has a bad reputation these days, especially among many Christians. Talk about providing an argument for the Christian faith, and someone may quote the apostle Paul:

> *The Lord's servant must not be quarrelsome but must be kind to everyone.*
> **2 TIMOTHY 2:24a**

This view is unfortunate because an argument does not need to be emotional at all. In other words, quarreling and arguing are two very different things. Properly defined, an argument is "a coherent series of reasons, statements, or facts intended to support or establish a point of view."[5] The classic example of a logical argument comes from introductory philosophy courses:

PREMISE 1: All men are mortal.
PREMISE 2: Socrates is a man.
CONCLUSION: Therefore, Socrates is mortal.

This is a sound logical argument. Arguments are not controversial; arguments are true or false, inaccurate or probable. Rather, it is the subject matter of arguments that can sometimes generate more heat than light.

How does this differ from the way you typically view arguments?

With arguments it is the delivery or the intent—often to illustrate why another person is mistaken—that triggers an emotional response. For this reason arguments must be presented graciously and respectfully, as Peter urged: "Do this with gentleness and respect" (1 Pet. 3:15). However, nothing is emotional or wrong about an argument itself.

What are some steps you can take to keep your emotions in check as you make an argument, especially when you are passionate about the subject?

GOD AND ARGUMENT

In the context of evangelism, many object: "You cannot argue someone into the kingdom of God." Scripture is very clear that new birth, eternal life, forgiveness of sins, and adoption into God's family are acts of God, not humans. Through the process of conversion, a person goes from spiritual death to spiritual life.

Arguments don't save people; this is a supernatural act of God. Still, arguments are important in removing intellectual barriers to faith in Christ.

Read the following passages and reflect on ways God approves of using argument to thoughtfully engage with others.

Job 38:1—42:6	Isaiah 1:18-20	2 Corinthians 10:5
What approach did God take in dealing with Job? How did Job respond?	When speaking to the Israelites and urging them to repent, what does God's invitation to "reason together" with Him suggest (v. 18, ESV)?	What is the significance of Paul's claim that "we demolish arguments" and "take captive every thought to make it obedient to Christ"?

THE EARLY CHURCH

Argument is just one approach the first disciples used to engage with their non-Christian neighbors. Read each verse and highlight the action verbs that describe the early believers' approach to contending for the gospel.

With many other words he warned them; and he pleaded with them, "Save yourselves from this corrupt generation."
ACTS 2:40

Day after day, in the temple courts and from house to house, they never stopped teaching and proclaiming the good news that Jesus is the Messiah.
ACTS 5:42

[Saul] talked and debated with the Hellenistic Jews, but they tried to kill him.
ACTS 9:29

The Berean Jews were of more noble character than those in Thessalonica, for they received the message with great eagerness and examined the Scriptures every day to see if what Paul said was true.
ACTS 17:11

[Paul] witnessed to them from morning till evening, explaining about the kingdom of God, and from the Law of Moses and from the Prophets he tried to persuade them about Jesus.
ACTS 28:23

What stands out to you in this list? Explain.

How do these Scriptures challenge your view of evangelism?

Why might evangelism include more than sharing a simple version of the gospel?

HISTORICAL TRUTH, NOT LEGEND

Not only did the early church value the importance of thoughtfully engaging with others on matters of truth, but it also valued faithfully preserving and transmitting important evidence about Christ. The clearest example of this effort is known as a creed, which consists of important truths compressed into as few words as possible. Creeds helped believers to teach young Christians and prepare to defend the faith from intellectual attack.

What are some biblical teachings that were passed down to you by older family members, church leaders, or Christian mentors?

The New Testament includes ancient creeds that already existed prior to its composition. Read 1 Corinthians 15:3-8 to see one of the most important creeds recorded by the apostle Paul.

> *What I received I passed on to you as of first importance: that Christ died for our sins according to the Scriptures. What I received I passed on to you as of first importance: that Christ died for our sins according to the Scriptures, that he was buried, that he was raised on the third day according to the Scriptures, and that he appeared to Cephas, and then to the Twelve. After that, he appeared to more than five hundred of the brothers and sisters at the same time, most of whom are still living, though some have fallen asleep. Then he appeared to James, then to all the apostles, and last of all he appeared to me also, as to one abnormally born.*
>
> **1 CORINTHIANS 15:3-8**

Paul most likely learned the creed from Peter and James during his visit to Jerusalem three years after his conversion (Gal. 1:18-19). Paul used the Greek term *historeo,* which means "to gain a historical account,"[6] to describe his visit with Peter (v. 18). Because many scholars date Paul's conversion between AD 31 and AD 33,[7] the creed would have been developed quite early.

We can safely conclude that the resurrection of Jesus is not a legendary development. Legends and myths take several generations to develop. Because the creed recorded in 1 Corinthians 15:3-8 was formed (at most) just a few years after Jesus' crucifixion, there was no possible way for legendary elements to creep in, because there was no time for this corruption to occur.

Equipped with this historical information, how could you respond to someone who claimed Jesus' resurrection is a legend that developed over time?

What other internal evidence does the Bible present about its reliability? What Scriptures would you point to?

Atheism and Scientism

START

In our first challenge to bring up your faith to someone who is not yet a Christian, we asked:

What is your biggest objection to Christianity?
What do you think it would take for you to change your mind about God and become a Christian?

Was the person willing to talk? Did you enjoy the conversation?

What were the most common objections?

What underlying experiences or concerns motivated each of their objections?

What did people say it would take for them to accept Christ?

Sometimes objections are linked to negative experiences people have had. Sometimes objections are linked to concerns about fairness or justice, for people to be treated lovingly, or for beliefs to be based on evidence. Sometimes even more important than finding the flaws in objections to faith is finding underlying points of agreement that can be starting points for further conversation.

Did you notice anything about the relationship between the answer to the first question and the answer to the second question? Explain.

As we hope to share Christ with those who do not know Him, we are not interested in winning debates just for the sake of it. We are interested in lovingly introducing people to the person of Jesus Christ and to what He has done for them.

THIS WEEK'S TOPIC

I love sports. But here is a sporting experience I would never want to have. Imagine being thrown into a game without knowing when it started, when it will finish, what the objective of the game is, or what the rules are. What would you do? You would probably ask the other players around you to answer those four questions for you.

What if they responded with many different answers? Or what if they simply carried on playing, uninterested in your questions and looking at you oddly for asking them? Next you would look to a coach for help, but what if the coach was looking at the chaos and yelling, "Great job, guys! You're all doing great! Keep going! We've got a first-place trophy waiting for all of you!"

Now imagine the conversations about the game on the drive home. They would be completely meaningless. It is our knowledge of the start, the finish, the objective, and the rules of a game that provides us with the freedom to play it and enjoy it in a meaningful way.

Sadly, this is not just a game; this is a reality for many who are struggling to live a meaningful life in our culture. As a society, we are losing the answers to these four crucial questions.

Origin: Where did I come from?
Meaning: Why am I here?
Morality: How should I live?
Destiny: Where am I going?

Your answers to those four fundamental questions form the basis of your worldview—the lens through which you experience and interpret the world around you—which influences the way you choose to live. We all need answers to the deepest questions of life.

Do you think Christianity or atheism does a better job of answering the four questions of origin, meaning, morality, and destiny? Why?

The number of Americans who identify as atheists has roughly doubled in recent years. Why do you think that is the case?

WATCH

Use this space to take notes as you watch the video for Week 2.

1. Faith and reason are not _____, but actually they're necessary for one another.

2. _____ without alternative is _____.

3. The _____ worldview critiques without offering any alternative.

4. How does _____ come from nothing?

5. With God, I can _____ numerous questions.

6. Without God, the most _____ questions are _____.

7. Everything that comes into _____ has a _____.

8. Science is not only _____ with the existence of God, but it actually _____ to the existence of God.

9. Nontheists and skeptics believe in a god of the _____.

10. When you talk about _____, you assume there's good; when you assume there's good, you assume there's a _____ _____.

11. Every question about evil is either raised by a _____, or about a person, which means the question assumes intrinsic _____ for personhood.

WORDS TO KNOW

Atheism: the view that there is no God
Scientism: the view that science can explain everything
Naturalist: someone who believes nothing has supernatural significance, but everything can be explained by science
Microcosm: a small part of a larger world or universe; epitome of a group or place
Macrocosm: the universe as a whole; large group made up of smaller groups (microcosms)

Answers: 1. opposed; 2. Criticism, empty; 3. atheist; 4. something; 5. answer; 6. fundamental, unanswerable; 7. effect, cause; 8. compatible, points; 9. gaps; 10. evil, moral law; 11. person, worth

DEBRIEF

The video suggests that atheism and scientism have trouble explaining reality.

What fundamental questions of life do atheism and scientism leave unanswered?

Do you think it takes more faith to be a Christian or to be an atheist? Why?

An atheist might say people who believe in God must prove He exists, rather than nonbelievers proving He doesn't. Richard Dawkins said it this way:

> *If you want to believe in ... unicorns, or tooth fairies, Thor or Yahweh—the onus is on you to say why you believe in it. The onus is not on the rest of us to say why we do not.*[1]

Do you agree with Dawkins' statement? Why or why not?

How do atheism and scientism subtly creep into the Christian life?

Many people have heard unfounded rumors that science has disproved God. Without thinking it through, they have jumped from science to scientism—from the welcome fact that science can explain a lot to the deeply problematic assumption that it can explain everything. In reality, science points to God.

How would you respond to someone who claims science explains everything and there is no need for God?

Read Psalm 19:1-2. How does the Bible answer the claims of scientism?

Even philosopher Immanuel Kant said two things fill the mind with awe: "the starry heavens above me and the moral law within me."[2] He echoed the Bible's affirmation that God's attributes "have been clearly perceived, ever since the creation of the world, in the things that have been made" (Rom. 1:20, ESV) and that God's law "is written on [people's] hearts, while their conscience also bears witness" (Rom. 2:15, ESV). Science and morality do not disprove God's existence; they point to Him.

While many believe science has disproved God, in fact only God proves science:

> *When you talk about evil, you assume there's good; when you assume good, you assume there is a moral law by which we differentiate between good and evil; and if you assume a moral law you must assume a moral lawgiver. If there's no moral lawgiver, there's no moral law; if there's no moral law, there's no good; if there's no good, there's no evil.*
>
> **RAVI ZACHARIAS**

Based on Ravi's statement, when someone raises a moral objection to God, what question could you ask to help show the tension underlying their objection?

PRAYER

- Read Psalm 8 aloud together and reflect on the way it progresses from wonder at God's creation, to an appreciation of God's grace, and finally to a response of worship.

BRINGING UP YOUR FAITH

Use the following questions to start a conversation with a non-believer this week.

As you share your faith this week, you'll ask a question that has the potential to lead to many deep, life-changing conversations about the Christian faith:

**Have you ever experienced something in your life
that made you think there might be a God?**

Feel free to ask the same person you talked with last week or talk to someone else. Allow the person time to reflect and respond, and then check your understanding by summarizing and repeating what the person said to you. Possible follow-up questions include:

Why did that experience make you think there might be a God?

**Have you experienced anything else that made you think there might
be a God?**

How does the idea of God's existence make you feel?

Would you like for God to exist? Why or why not?

Remember to pray about your conversation in advance. Keep in mind that God is sovereign over all your interactions. These talks are divine appointments, both for you and the person you talk with.

JOURNAL

Use this page to reflect on your conversation.

Whom did you talk with? What was your overall experience with this conversation?

How willing was the person to have a conversation with you? What obstacles did you encounter?

What insights did you gain about communicating truth with gentleness and respect?

SCIENCE AND GOD

Imagine you're grabbing coffee with a friend, and as you talk, he says to you, "There's just no scientific evidence for God's existence. That's why I'm an atheist. Religious belief is unscientific, so why should I believe in God?"

How would you respond?

DEFINING SCIENCE

How would you define the word *science*?

Consider the following definitions of *science*.

[Science] by definition deals only with the natural, the repeatable, that which is governed by law.[3]
MICHAEL RUSE

The essence of true science is a willingness to follow empirical evidence, wherever it leads.[4]
JOHN LENNOX

How does your definition compare with these two definitions? To which definition is yours most similar?

What stands out to you in these two definitions? Which definition is broader, and which is narrower? Which definition immediately excludes God from the realm of science?

THE COMPATIBILITY OF GOD AND SCIENCE

History reveals that there is no conflict between God and science. The vast majority of prominent scientists throughout history were theists; most of them were actually Christians. Rather than being an obstacle to their science, their belief in God was a major inspiration for it.[5]

For example, Johannes Kepler (1571–1630)—who formulated the laws of planetary motion—said his motivation was "to discover the rational order which has been imposed on [the universe] by God, and which he revealed to us in the language of mathematics."[6] Therefore, the idea that God and science are in conflict or incompatible should be recognized for the misleading claim that it is.

What does Kepler's example suggest to you about the possibility of being a Christian who believes in both God and the value of science? Has this ever caused tension for you?

How does science enhance your belief in God? Why is it unhelpful and unnecessary to think about God and science as mutually exclusive?

THE GENERAL CREATED ORDER POINTS TO GOD

The Bible has much to say about what we can infer from observing the world around us. Lennox's advice to follow the evidence reveals five features of the created order that present a significant problem for atheism but are explained by the biblical worldview.

Feature 1: The universe had a beginning.
The Issue: Science and philosophy affirm that the universe had a beginning, but can atheism account for the change from nothing to something?

As recent scientific and philosophical evidence affirms, the universe had a beginning and has not existed eternally, contrary to Aristotle's view that dominated scientific thinking for centuries.[7] In other words, the available academic evidence reveals that everything—matter, energy, space, and time—came into existence *ex nihilo*, or "out of nothing."

Science and philosophy do not supply all the evidence. Read the following passages to see what the Bible says about the creation of the universe.

In the beginning God created
the heavens and the earth.
GENESIS 1:1

*The heavens declare the glory of God; the skies
proclaim the work of his hands.*
PSALM 19:1

*By faith we understand that the universe was
formed at God's command, so that what is seen was
not made out of what was visible.*
HEBREWS 11:3

Ultimately, science and philosophy have simply confirmed what the Bible has clearly affirmed for centuries. Robert Jastrow, a former NASA astronomer, humorously summarized the point:

*For the scientist who has lived by his faith in the
power of reason, the story ends like a bad dream.
He has scaled the mountains of ignorance; he is
about to conquer the highest peak; as he pulls
himself over the final rock, he is greeted by a
band of theologians who have been sitting there
for centuries.*[8]

Atheism has no answer for the creation of something from nothing. For the atheist, the universe is all there is, and it cannot create itself. God possesses the necessary attributes to create a universe like ours.

- God is immaterial: "God is spirit" (John 4:24).
- God is eternal: "Stand up and praise the LORD your God, who is from everlasting to everlasting" (Neh. 9:5).
- God is all-powerful: "I am the LORD, the God of all mankind. Is anything too hard for me?" (Jer. 32:27).

Things do not just pop into existence for no reason. The best explanation is that the cause of the universe is something highly powerful and highly creative from outside space, and it is difficult to think of a better candidate for that description than God.

How does reflecting on God's character and attributes lead us to appreciate the way the world has been made?

Why is God the best and most believable explanation for the beginning of the universe?

Feature 2: The universe is finely tuned for life.
The Issue: Can atheists explain the fine-tuning of the universe by random chance?

Saying the universe is finely tuned for life means that a universe as complex as ours meets all the conditions necessary to sustain life. Even committed atheists have admitted that the fine-tuning argument is an effective argument against atheism. The fact that the universe is so finely tuned for life—to such a precise degree that it defies comprehension—cries out for explanation. And a convincing explanation is exactly what the Bible provides.

Consider the descriptions the following verses provide for how God established the universe.

- **Job 38:33**
- **Psalm 19:1**
- **Psalm 136:5**
- **Isaiah 45:18**
- **Hebrews 11:3**

Atheism can explain the amazing fine-tuning of our universe only by appealing either to random (and unlikely) chance or to an unsupported metaphysical guess, such as the multiverse. However, as the previous verses show, the Bible offers a much more believable explanation for why our universe would be so perfectly suited for life. They reveal an ultimate purpose to our universe: In His love and wisdom, God established the laws of the heavens by working, forming, commanding, and ordering our universe so we could inhabit it.

metaphysical: philosophical concept that involves the transcendent or describes the basic essence of reality and existence

multiverse: You may also hear this called a parallel universe. Essentially, the multiverse theory suggests that our universe may be one of many.

How do God's intentionality and purpose support the evidence from science about the fine-tuning of the universe?

How could the order and function we see in the world around us provide a way for you to begin a conversation about God with an unbeliever?

GOD'S FINGERPRINTS

For this study, we pick up where the first study left off.

Feature 3: The universe is regular.

The Issue: How do we explain that the universe has carried on with regularity, and why do we assume that it will continue to do so in the future?

The universe should operate in a regular manner, with absolute predictability day after day. This may seem like an obvious observation, but the uniformity of nature requires a good explanation.

What regular patterns have you observed in the world around you?

What conclusions can you make about the world based on these observations?

Ultimately, scientists accept the uniformity of nature as a matter of faith. As physicist Paul Davies commented:

> *Just because the sun has risen every day of your life, there is no guarantee that it will rise tomorrow. The belief that it will—that there are indeed dependable regularities of nature—is an act of faith, but one which is indispensable to the progress of science.*[9]

For Christians, this act of faith is reasonable, because it is based on the character of God, who cares for us and wants us to live orderly and meaningful lives.

Read Colossians 1:17 and Hebrews 1:3. How do these verses describe the way God maintains the regularity of the universe?

Without a being like God—one who sustains creation at all moments and in whom all things hold together—atheists have no explanation for why the universe has always operated with such regularity and will continue doing so. From a naturalistic viewpoint, it is a great mystery. The only adequate explanation for the regularity of the universe is God.

Why is a regular universe necessary for us to live orderly and meaningful lives?

Feature 4: The universe is knowable.
The Issue: Atheistic evolution aims at survival, not truth. Why assume our beliefs are in any way reliable?

Albert Einstein remarked:

The most incomprehensible thing about the universe is that it is comprehensible. ... One should expect a chaotic world, which cannot be grasped by the mind in any way.[10]

The success humans have experienced in discovering and understanding the universe is completely surprising to atheists, because atheism is not aimed at truth, but focuses on how people behave to survive. In contrast, the knowable nature of the universe and the ability of human minds to explore its workings are completely consistent with the picture of humanity we see in the Bible.

The Bible is absolutely clear that humanity is a miraculous, special act of creation, not the result of a blind, unguided evolutionary process. The Bible specifically affirms three important truths about each of us.

1. We are made in the image of God (Gen. 1:26-27; 2:7; 5:1-2). God is a rational being; therefore we are also rational beings. This means we have good reason to trust our minds to guide us to what is true.
2. Each of us is "fearfully and wonderfully made" (Ps. 139:14). We are created beings, not cosmic accidents.
3. "We are God's handiwork" (Eph. 2:10). Each of us was created for a purpose, and therefore God has filled our lives with dignity and meaning.

Which of these three truths most often leads you to praise God? Why?

The Bible suggests that rather than reveal all knowledge to us in advance, God chose to leave the discovery to us because He delights in our exploration of the universe. Like a loving parent, God is pleased by our wonder and amazement that result from exploring His creation:

> *Great are the works of the LORD;*
> *they are pondered by all who delight in them.*
> **PSALM 111:2**

> *It is the glory of God to conceal a matter;*
> *to search out a matter is the glory of kings.*
> **PROVERBS 25:2**

How does the existence of our minds and our ability to discover establish evidence against atheism and in favor of theism?

Feature 5: The universe is moral.
The Issue: How can someone ground morality in something other than God?

There seems to be a moral law within each of us. While any number of factors—culture, sin, drugs, abuse, or mental illness—can change or suppress our moral reasoning, it appears we have a natural ability to engage in meaningful moral reasoning. Consider these examples:

- "My argument against God was that the universe seemed so cruel and unjust. But how had I got this idea of just and unjust? What was I comparing this universe with when I called it unjust?"[11] —C. S. Lewis

- "We hold these truths to be self-evident, that all men are created equal, that they are endowed by their Creator with certain unalienable Rights, that among these are Life, Liberty and the pursuit of Happiness."[12] —The Declaration of Independence

- "All human beings are born free and equal in dignity and rights. They are endowed with reason and conscience and should act towards one another in a spirit of brotherhood."[13] —The Universal Declaration of Human Rights

How closely does the vision of morality presented in these statements align with what you read in the Bible?

Consider your non-believing friends. On what do they base their idea of right and wrong?

Our governments, our laws, and our inner conscience declare that we are moral beings. But what explains this fact? According to atheistic thinkers Michael Ruse and Richard Dawkins, morality is an unpredictable and deceptive evolutionary by-product. Still, we continue to make moral judgments about good or bad behaviors. The Bible explains why this is so. Consider the way the following two verses address morality and the human heart.

> *[Gentiles] show that the requirements of the law*
> *are written on their hearts, their consciences*
> *also bearing witness, and their thoughts*
> *sometimes accusing them and at other times even*
> *defending them.*
> **ROMANS 2:15**

> *The heart is deceitful above all things and beyond*
> *cure. Who can understand it?*
> **JEREMIAH 17:9**

Each verse reveals an important truth. First, morality is not grounded in human reason. Rather, we use reason to discern the moral law God has written on our hearts. Second, no amount of secular human reasoning will take us to morality, because the human heart is warped by sin and beyond the ability of any human (but not God) to repair.

Some atheists certainly attempt to bypass these conclusions using science. But science cannot answer the deep moral questions of life. There are two clear reasons for this reality.

1. Using science to answer moral questions is a category mistake. As John Lennox remarks:

> *Science can tell you that, if you add strychnine to someone's drink, it will kill them. But science cannot tell you whether it is morally right or wrong to put strychnine into your grandmother's tea so that you can get your hands on her property.*[14]

2. A moral law requires a moral lawgiver:

> *An impersonal force won't do because a moral rule encompasses both a proposition and a command; both are features of minds.*[15]

The moral convictions of justice, love, and mercy make sense only when communicated from one person to another; such convictions lose meaning when not attached to a person (or moral authority). And that person must be a personal God whose character provides an absolute standard of goodness.

Therefore, the moral law is ultimately grounded in the person of God and comes from His character. As God told the Israelites, "Be holy because I, the LORD your God, am holy" (Lev. 19:2).

Read 1 Corinthians 2:14. If there are limits to what scientific data can tell us about reality, then what are the risks of using a scientific approach in all aspects of our walk with God?

Why is it important to leave room for the spiritual as well as observations based on science?

Equipped with this information, how could you respond to your friend who asserted that science and belief in God are incompatible?

In what ways do you need to adjust your own thinking about science and belief of God?

Pluralism

START

We hope in the past week you had the chance to ask someone the following:

**Have you ever experienced something in your life
that made you think there might be a God?**

How did the person respond?

What can we learn from the answers we received?

What would you do differently if you had the same conversation again?

Would you ask that question again? Why or why not?

How could you revise, adapt, or add to this question if you ask it again?

THIS WEEK'S TOPIC

"All views are equally valid." This is the form of pluralism we will discuss this week. It claims that although our opinions about the deep questions of life may seem different on the surface, they are actually fundamentally the same or at least fundamentally of equal worth.

The logical problems with this view surface almost immediately. Does the view that all views *are* equally valid also apply to the view that all views are *not* equally valid?

RZIM speaker Abdu Murray had a conversation with a student who said he did not think it was his place to disagree with anyone. Abdu responded, "Sure you do." The student replied, "No, I don't." Abdu said, "You just did."

Vince had a related conversation with a student who said, "I think there is a universal human longing for peace, and I think that points to the reality of something that can fulfill that longing, sort of like how hunger points to the reality of food." To that point, Vince followed him. But then he concluded, "So I think it's a good idea to believe in something, whatever that is." The student assumed all big picture worldviews would meet this universal human need more or less equally well.

What secular gods do people worship? Why don't those gods bring peace?

What would have to be true of a worldview for it to provide ultimate peace?

As we discussed in Week 2, as important as it is for us to find flaws in mistaken worldviews, it is often even more important to find points of agreement that can act as starting points for conversation and relationship.

What are some good and honest motivations that lead to belief in pluralism? Why are people attracted to it?

Why do you think our society is happy to judge right and wrong when it comes to what we put in our bodies, but refuses to judge right and wrong with respect to what we put in our minds and souls?

WATCH

Use this space to take notes as you watch the video for Week 3.

1. Reasoning is built upon the fundamental laws of _____, and the laws of logic ultimately underlie _____.

2. You have to have a _____ _____ _____ for absolute thinking.

3. Pluralism in _____, in _____, in _____—wonderful.

4. Pluralism in logic ultimately leads to a _____, accident-oriented world.

5. We're afraid of truth because truth leads to _____, and we don't know how to _____ anymore.

6. You either flee from truth toward _____ or you fight for truth and lose all _____.

7. At the cross, we see God's greatest _____ with us and—at the very same moment—we see God's greatest _____ for us.

8. Love without _____ is not _____.
   Truth without _____ is not _____.

9. The question is not whether they are different or not, the question is which of these is _____ and deals with the reality of _____.

10. All these realities are the outflow of He not just _____ the truth, but He _____ the truth.

WORDS TO KNOW
Pluralism: the view that all views are equally valid
Law of Non-contradiction: contradictory statements can't both be true without qualifying one of them
Post-truth Culture: a culture which is no longer shaped by absolute truth or objective facts; instead, it is shaped by opinion and emotion

Answers: 1. logic, reality; 2. point of reference; 3. aesthetics, tastes, foods; 4. chaotic; 5. disagreement, disagree; 6. pluralism, civility; 7. disagreement, love 8. truth, love, love, truth; 9. true, truth; 10. speaking, being

DEBRIEF

The Perceived Trajectory of Truth

Truth $\Rightarrow$ Disagreement $\Rightarrow$ Devaluing $\Rightarrow$ Intolerance $\Rightarrow$ Extremism $\Rightarrow$ Violence $\Rightarrow$ Terrorism

In the video, Ravi and Vince talked about the nature of disagreement. When you are faced with disagreement, is your instinct to fight or flee? In what ways?

What is positive about your reaction? What is negative about it?

Where do you see examples in our culture of love at the expense of truth or truth at the expense of love?

$$GOD = LOVE$$
$$GOD = TRUTH$$
$$\overline{TRUTH = LOVE}$$

Jesus on the cross is simultaneously the greatest act of God's disagreement with us and the greatest act of God's love for us. Only in Jesus does truth equal love; therefore, only Jesus can get us out of the cultural ultimatum we are stuck in: choosing to fight or flee. Every other worldview makes a choice between love and truth. Jesus refused to make that choice, because only in Him are love and truth the same.

What real life examples of holding love and truth together in unity have you experienced or heard about?

As Christians, what would it look like for us to express our disagreement with others in our act of sacrificial love for them, like Jesus did for us?

One misconception that can lead to pluralism is the assumption that, at the end of the day, most of the major worldviews are pretty much the same. On the contrary, the world's major worldviews are fundamentally different and only superficially similar.

If someone asked you to identify three key unique features of Christianity, what would you choose? Why?

How has Christianity made a practical difference in your life? How does this difference demonstrate the uniqueness of Christianity?

PRAYER

In the Bible, God consistently admonishes us to let only Him be God.

- Read Leviticus 19:4; Deuteronomy 6:13-14; and Isaiah 40:25-26, and allow these verses to guide your prayer.

- As a group, spend some time confessing when we have put our trust or found our identity in anyone or anything other than God. Declare that He is our one and only God and Savior.

BRINGING UP YOUR FAITH

Use the following questions to engage with a non-believer this week.

Perhaps the most unique aspect of the Christian faith is God's unconditional love for every person. This is often one of the most challenging Christian beliefs for people to accept, because many people—both Christians and non-Christians—struggle to believe that they are lovable and that they are loved.

This week, as you share your faith with someone who is not a Christian, ask the following:

If God exists, what do you think He thinks of you?

This question can often expose that the God someone is rejecting is not the God of the Christian faith. Some people may respond by saying they think God is indifferent toward them or by talking about what God would think of the way they have recently behaved. There may be truth in this second response, but the question is not about what God thinks of their behavior but what God thinks of *them*.

Asking this question can provide an opportunity to share with people that—although God may be pleased or displeased with various aspects of their behavior—God loves them, He thinks of them as His beloved creation, and He longs to be in relationship with them.

In our broken world of disappointments and shattered dreams, it is a gift to be able to share with people that they are deeply loved.

The story of the prodigal son (Luke 15)—who did everything wrong but was still extravagantly loved by his father and invited back into relationship with him—may be a powerful story to share with those who do not know about God's universal, unconditional love.

JOURNAL

Use this page to reflect on your conversation.

Whom did you talk with? What was your overall experience with this conversation?

How willing was the person to have a conversation with you? What obstacles did you encounter?

What insights did you gain about communicating truth with gentleness and respect?

THE EXCLUSIVITY OF TRUTH

Imagine you are having dinner with a friend who says: "Christianity just seems arrogant. I mean, think about it. When Christians claim their beliefs are true and Jesus is the only way to God, they're saying everyone else is wrong. That's so narrow-minded! Where's the humility in telling others how wrong they are?"

How would you respond?

E PLURIBUS UNUM

The traditional motto of the United States is the Latin expression *e pluribus unum*, meaning "out of many, one." In many cases, plurality is a good thing. At its best, America's society is a wonderful human tapestry woven together from the lives of millions of people with different languages, music, food, literature, art, and ethnicities.

Furthermore, diversity is an ideal that God values. Consider the way the apostle John described his supernatural vision of heaven:

> *After this I looked, and there before me was a great*
> *multitude that no one could count, from every*
> *nation, tribe, people and language, standing before*
> *the throne and before the Lamb. They were wearing*
> *white robes and were holding palm branches in*
> *their hands.*
> **REVELATION 7:9**

According to God's own revelation, every "nation, tribe, people and language" will be represented in heaven. Heaven will be the place where those "out of many" who have placed their trust in Jesus Christ will come together to worship the One.

The ethnicity of each person is sacred because ethnicity is an essential, unchangeable component of personhood, and each person is made in God's image. It is no surprise that heaven, the place where God will dwell with His people forever (Rev. 21:3), reflects the diversity of His image bearers.

In what ways does Christianity embrace diversity?

How should diversity affect our understanding of the Great Commission (Matt. 28:18-20; Acts 1:8)?

DISAGREEING WITHOUT BEING DISAGREEABLE

People are not the same as beliefs. It is incredibly important not to confuse the reality of a pluralistic society (a society that includes people of diverse beliefs) with being pluralistic about truth. The former is good because all people are equally valuable; the latter is irrational and should be rejected.

Unlike people—who are intrinsically valuable because they bear the image of God—beliefs are simply true or false. What makes a belief valuable or valid is whether it is true. In other words, beliefs that are true and strongly supported by evidence are preferable to those that are false and lacking in evidence.

In your own words, describe the difference between being pluralistic in culture and being pluralistic in truth.

It is tempting to want to affirm all beliefs as equally valid in order to be inclusive and avoid the risk of offending friends, family members, or classmates. This fear is understandable; no one wants to be viewed as narrow-minded, stuck-up, intolerant, or biased. But affirming all beliefs as equally valid results in two mistakes.

1. It confuses a person with his or her beliefs. Criticizing a belief, if done respectfully, is not the same as criticizing the person who holds that belief.

2. Affirming all beliefs as equally valuable is, for all practical purposes, equivalent to claiming that all ideas are equally right, equally correct, or equally true.

While Christians should always heed biblical warnings to disagree without being rude (Col. 4:6; 1 Pet. 3:15), we are called to disagree when false ideas are being passed off as true.

Read the following passages and consider the instructions Paul gave early church leaders for correcting error and following truth.
- **1 Timothy 4:16**
- **2 Timothy 4:3**
- **Titus 1:9**

What are some ways we could put these commands into practice today?

As these verses demonstrate, Paul clearly thought some beliefs were more valuable than others because they were true, and "knowledge of the truth ... leads to godliness" (Titus 1:1). Therefore, Paul encouraged his readers to correct, rebuke, warn, and encourage others and to respond to unsound teaching and false doctrine with the truth.

But don't miss the fact that Paul also encouraged them to do so "with great patience and careful instruction" (2 Tim. 4:2) because God's servants must be "kind to everyone" and "not resentful" (2 Tim. 2:24). Paul was teaching his young leaders the important skill of disagreeing without being rude.

Read John 15:18-20; Romans 12:14; and 2 Timothy 3:12.

Even though the exclusivity of Jesus' claims can upset other people, why should we still share them anyway?

JESUS IS THE TRUTH

Why emphasize valuing truth? Because the same God who values the plurality of human diversity flatly rejects the notion of pluralism about truth itself. In Scripture, we see this fact in two primary ways.

1. Jesus said He is "the way and the truth and the life" (John 14:6). Notice Jesus did not just claim to be someone who speaks or teaches the truth; He claimed to be truth itself, incarnated in human form (Phil. 2:5-11). Therefore, everything Jesus said and did is true and authoritative.

2. Jesus followed up this statement with another: "No one comes to the Father except through me" (John 14:6). The early church was just as clear on this point. Consider the following statements by Jesus and His apostles:

- Jesus: "This is eternal life: that they know you, the only true God, and Jesus Christ, whom you have sent" (John 17:3).

- Peter: "Salvation is found in no one else, for there is no other name under heaven given to mankind by which we must be saved" (Acts 4:12).

- John: "Whoever has the Son has life; whoever does not have the Son of God does not have life" (1 John 5:12).

- Paul: "There is one God and one mediator between God and mankind, the man Christ Jesus" (1 Tim. 2:5).

Therefore, despite all the options in the marketplace of religions, not all paths lead to God (or claim to). Eternal life and salvation—intimate, loving relationship with God—are found in Christ alone and no one else (Rev. 3:20).

Why do you think this truth makes people uncomfortable?

The exclusivity of this claim rubs many people the wrong way. However, truth is exclusive by definition, because what is true must logically exclude its opposite. As Ravi explained:

> *The gospel of Jesus Christ is beautiful and true,*
> *yet oftentimes one will ask, "How can it be true*
> *that there is only one way?" Odd, isn't it, that we*
> *don't ask the same questions of the laws of nature*
> *or of any assertion that lays claim to truth. We are*
> *discomfited by the fact that truth, by definition, is*
> *exclusive. That is what truth claims are at their core.*
> *To make an assertion is to deny its opposite.*[1]

How does sharing even difficult truths express love?

If Jesus, Peter, Paul, and John's statements are all true, then no other person—including Mohammed, Buddha, Confucius, or oneself—can provide eternal life or salvation. Only Jesus can do that.

What is the relationship between our sinful hearts and our denial of truth?

Why should the exclusivity of Jesus delight and not disappoint us?

Before you came to Christ, what truth claims of Christianity were difficult for you to accept? How did you ultimately accept them?

CHRISTIANITY AND THE TESTS FOR TRUTH

KNOWING TRUTH

There are three tests for truth a worldview must satisfy in order to be credible.

1. **A worldview must be logically consistent**, meaning its teachings cannot be self-contradictory. This first test is critical because it excludes worldviews that are ultimately irrational or contradict themselves.

2. **A worldview must be empirically adequate.** In other words, its teachings must match what we see in reality. Without this criterion, we may end up believing a logically consistent fairy tale.

3. **A worldview must be existentially relevant.** A worldview's teachings must speak directly to questions of meaning and the way we actually live our lives; otherwise, we have only an academic theory and not an effective way of viewing the world.

THE MOTIVATIONS OF PLURALISM

Three good, God-given desires commonly motivate pluralism.

1. **Equal value.** Pluralism can be motivated by a commitment to the equal value of every person.

2. **Equal opportunity.** Pluralism can be motivated by fairness. People should have equal access to the truth or equal opportunity to discover the truth.

3. **Equal unity.** Pluralism can be motivated by a longing for unity and community.

However, pluralism applied to religious truth is ultimately flawed. While these legitimate motivations find only a partial and distorted fulfillment in pluralism, they are completely fulfilled by Christ in a way that satisfies all three tests for truth. Let's consider each motivation individually.

Motivation 1: Equal Value. One reason people turn to pluralism is the good desire that all people should be valued. However, in Christianity all people have natural worth and value. All people are loved by God, not just the people who have chosen to follow Him.

Read the following Scriptures and record what they teach about God's love for you.

- **Matthew 10:29-31**

- **John 3:16**

- **Romans 5:8, 8:38-39**

As our colleague Abdu Murray explained, God's love, Jesus' sacrifice, and our inherent value are inseparably bound together:

> *The incarnation and the cross are profound demonstrations of the value we have in God's eyes and of our inherent dignity. They tell us that our actions are significant because they have consequences. And they tell us that God must address those consequences, but in a way that saves us from ourselves—because he values us. ... At the cross God paid an infinite price to show our infinite value. As a triune being, he does not need relationship with us to have relationship. He has it within himself in the eternal community of the Trinity.[2]*

God's love is the one and only thing that is equal for every person. As the apostle Paul made clear, God's love never changes and cannot be lost. In the end, human value is personal and measured by the love of a personal God "who did not spare his own Son, but gave him up for us all" (Rom. 8:32).

How does it affect you to know that your value is measured by God's love for you?

The Christian narrative about God's love and our value satisfy the tests for truth. Because God is the Trinity, Jesus the Son could pay the penalty for our sin by dying on the cross. The divine transaction of substitutionary atonement between the Son and the Father was very real. Further, the events of Jesus' death and resurrection can be verified through historical inquiry.

Finally, Jesus is existentially unique among the founders of major world religions. Jesus offers us rest from our troubles; He bears our burdens; He comes to us and rescues us; He provides salvation as a free gift; and unlike the founder of every other belief system, He lovingly takes our guilt on Himself. Jesus journeys through life with us, sustaining us along the way.

How does God's love for us in Christ make Christianity distinct from other belief systems?

Motivation 2: Equal Opportunity. A second admirable motivation for pluralism is a desire for all people to have access to the truth, yet God has already provided this opportunity to all people.

Read the following Scriptures, and record what they teach about God's desire to have a relationship with us.

You will seek me and find me when you seek me with all your heart.
JEREMIAH 29:13

Yet to all who did receive him, to those who believed in his name, he gave the right to become children of God.

JOHN 1:12

Here I am! I stand at the door and knock. If anyone hears my voice and opens the door, I will come in and eat with that person, and they with me.

REVELATION 3:20

The gospel has spread throughout much of the world, and there is even evidence of the presence of Christians in China as early as AD 86.[3] We certainly do not know everything about the ways God reveals Himself. However, we can be sure of this: All who want Him will find Him.

Though Christianity is often accused of being too narrow, why is it actually more open than pluralism?

Have you ever believed Christianity to be too narrow? Why? What made you think this way?

God's standards for entering the kingdom are extremely fair. As pastor Andy Stanley asked:

> What could be fairer than this? Everybody is welcome. Everybody gets in the same way. Everybody can meet the requirement.[4]

In other words, Jesus' starting point is everyone else's finish line—the assurance of salvation (John 5:24; Rom. 10:9; 1 John 5:13).

Here, the claims of Christianity once again pass the tests for truth. There is nothing logically inconsistent with God's promise to reveal Himself to those who seek Him, because it is God Himself who planted eternity in the hearts of people. As Augustine said:

> You have made us for yourself, O Lord, and our hearts are restless until they find their rest in you.[5]

We see this reality confirmed by the way God has made the gospel known throughout the centuries to various people groups all over the world. Finally, through the presence of God, who is always near, the deepest longings of our hearts are satisfied.

Motivation 3: Equal Unity. A final motivation for pluralism is a longing for unity with other people. Yet, we see that God's purpose for us is to be in community as He has been in eternal community with the Persons of the Trinity: Father, Son, and Holy Spirit. From eternity past God has existed in community.

As Christians, we discover a unity of diversity in the community of the Trinity. As theologian William G. T. Shedd explained:

> God is not a unit, but a unity. ... God is blessed
> only as he is self-knowing and self-communing.
> A subject without an object could not experience
> either love or joy. Love and joy are social.
> They imply more than a single person.[6]

The three trinitarian Persons love one another (John 3:35), dwell in one another (John 14:10-11), know one another (Matt. 11:27), address one another (Heb. 1:8), glorify one another (John 17:5), confer with one another (Gen. 1:26; 11:7), plan with one another (Isa. 9:6), send one another (John 14:26), and reward one another (Phil. 2:5-11; Heb. 2:9). God is very much a being in relationship!

While the concept of a triune being exceeds our full comprehension, there is nothing contradictory in claiming that God is one being (one *what*) and three Persons (three *whos*), because personhood and essence are separate categories.

And while the Trinity is disclosed only by special revelation from God rather than by natural theology, Jesus' revelation as the Son of God is confirmed by His resurrection from the dead (Acts 17:31).

Finally, it makes sense that we would also hunger for unity and community, because these things characterize the God whose image we bear. The community we long for reflects the perfect eternal community of the Trinity, and communion with God awaits us in heaven (Rev. 21:3).

Pluralism has become a prevalent worldview. For questions of theological truth, why is it important to remember that we are strangers in this world (Rom. 12:1-2; 1 Pet. 2:11)?

When have you been guilty of treating different worldviews as if they are equally valid? Explain. How has pluralism crept into the way you evaluate the world?

Having completed this week's personal studies, how would you respond differently to your pluralistic friend (p. 52)?

WEEK 4

Humanism and Relativism

START

Based on your conversations last week, discuss what people said in response to the following question:

If God exists, what do you think He thinks of you?

How did your conversation proceed from there?

What do these conversations tell us about the ways people view God?

What do these conversations tell us about the ways people view themselves?

Would you ask this question again if you had the opportunity? Why or why not?

If so, how might you change it or add to it?

THIS WEEK'S TOPIC

The word *relativism* is thrown around frequently today. While relativism takes a variety of forms, the basic idea is that truth is not the same for all of us. We are told to pursue our own truth and to be true to ourselves. We are told that all truth is relative to the individual, and therefore maybe what the Bible says about Jesus is true for you but not for me.

But there is a clear problem with saying, "All truth is relative." Does that include the truth that all truth is relative? If so, then what reason do I have to believe you when you tell me that all truth is relative? Maybe even that truth is true for you but not for me.

When have you heard someone say, "that's true for you, but not for me"?

Relativism about morality is especially frightening and devastating for society. How can we trust one another when a grave evil committed against you or your family can be justified with the words "It may have been evil for you, but it was not evil for me."

Relativism naturally leads to humanism. Relativism claims we can create our own truth, morality, and meaning on an individual level. Humanism—at least in its atheistic form—claims humanity can create its own value, meaning, and purpose as a society. In other words, humanism claims it is up to humanity to save itself.

Have you seen relativism or humanism in any of your conversations? What examples come to mind?

What are some examples of relativistic or humanistic influence on today's culture?

If humanism becomes the dominant worldview, how do you think that will influence the future of society?

WATCH

Use this space to take notes as you watch the video for Week 4.

1. We do not give the privilege of relativism to the _____ worldview; we only want it for ourselves.

2. The day we played _____, we actually _____.

3. We buried the truth, and in the process buried _____ itself.

4. You cannot live _____ in this world and still find _____.

5. Relativism is the handmaid of humanism because man becomes the _____ of all things, but nobody tells you _____ man.

6. Part of humanism is the mantra of _____.

7. The _____ at which real life begins for each of us is the burying of one's own _____ and self-sufficiency.

8. The human heart wrestles with pride: We don't like to admit _____ we are, how _____ we are, or how _____ we are.

9. See your heart as God sees your heart. When you see your heart as God sees your heart, you actually see what He has provided for you in the _____.

WORDS TO KNOW

Relativism: all truth is relative—what's true for you is true for you and what's true for me is true for me
Humanism: the belief that we can make progress on our own

Answers: 1. opposing; 2. God, died; 3. reason; 4. just, meaning; 5. measure, which; 6. progress; 7. funeral, pride; 8. who, vile, lost; 9. cross

DEBRIEF

Secular humanism believes we can look to human advancement for justice, peace, and the end of suffering—it is guided by the idea of progress.

Do you think we are making progress as a society? Why or why not?

Early humanists were Christians motivated by their belief that God gave human beings value, but today's atheistic humanism elevates human value and ethics while rejecting God.

Any plausible ethical theory acknowledges the equal value of every person. But for every person to be equally valuable, something must be equally true of every person. Humanism bases itself on human value but has cut itself off from the source of human value.

If God did not exist, what (if anything) would be equally true of every person?

How does being made in the image of God give all people inherent and equal value?

Humanism sees self-reliance as an ultimate virtue. The Bible depicts self-reliance as the original sin. The first humans could not resist the temptation to "be like God" (Gen. 3:5). As the notorious atheist Friedrich Nietzsche put it, "If there were gods, how could I bear not to be a God?"[1]

In sharp contrast to ultimately relying on ourselves, Christianity teaches that the only way for us to truly live is to remove ourselves from the equation. Real life begins for each of us when we bury our own pride and self-sufficiency. Self-reliance or God-reliance is the life-defining choice every heart has to make.

How has self-reliance failed you?

Humanism can be attractive to people who sense that eternity is written on their hearts (Eccl. 3:11) and recognize the human need for meaning, value, purpose, and hope but have turned away from Christianity because they have misconceptions about who God is.

What are the most common misconceptions about God that you have encountered?

How have Christians sometimes furthered misconceptions about God?

How does humanism creep into the Christian life? What do we say or do that is more humanist than Christian?

Sometimes humanism tricks us into seeing people as good people who are making progress on their own and just need to work hard to get a bit better, rather than as sinners in need of a Savior.

How would our lives look different if we really believed humanity is headed for spiritual death and desperately needs to be rescued?

PRAYER

- Read Proverbs 3:5-6 together.

- As you pray about the conversations you will have this week, ask God to help you lean completely on Him and trust that He will make your paths straight.

BRINGING UP YOUR FAITH

Use the following questions to start a conversation with a non-believer this week.

During the past few weeks, we have focused on asking good questions and being good listeners, which allows us to learn about people in a way that develops deeper trust and relationships. Often when we ask good questions, listen well, and build trust, we will have an opportunity to share our faith.

This week, ask:

Would you mind if I explained the central message of Christianity to you?

Write out the Christian message in your own words. As you write, it may help to imagine that you are writing a letter to share the gospel with your best friend. Then, sit down with the person you are explaining the central Christian message to, and read through what you have written together. Consider these follow-up questions:

What, if anything, about this message did you find difficult or confusing? What, if anything, was new or surprising to you?

What questions do you have about what I shared?

Christians can sometimes forget that things that seem clear to us may not be clear to people who are not used to thinking in Christian categories or language. These conversations will help us see ways we are being unclear, and they will give us opportunities to treat people with respect by asking to learn from their perspectives.

As we prepare to share the Christian message with a friend, family member, or classmate, we need God. He must be the One to lead us to the right person; to prepare that person's heart; and to give us His love for that person, His words to share, and faith and courage to trust Him as we make ourselves vulnerable in this way, remembering that Jesus made Himself vulnerable for us.

JOURNAL

Use this page to reflect on your conversation.

Whom did you talk with? What was your overall experience with this conversation?

How willing was the person to have a conversation with you? What obstacles did you encounter?

What insights did you gain about communicating truth with gentleness and respect?

HUMANISM

Imagine that a classmate said, "Why do we even need God? I mean, what purpose does He serve? Look at the world around us. There are lots of people like me who don't believe in God, but we're not bad people."

How would you respond?

HUMANITY IN THE DRIVER'S SEAT

Self-driving cars are often in the media these days. When reading news articles, you may come across the word *autonomous*, as in "autonomous self-driving cars." The description is appropriate because *autonomous* comes from the Greek words *auto* (*self*) and *nomos* (*law*). In other words, these cars are self-governed and independent in a way that excludes the need for human direction.

The Bible is clear that when it comes to God, human beings want to be just like these cars, only more so. As C. S. Lewis wrote:

> *Fallen man is not simply an imperfect creature who needs improvement: he is a rebel who must lay down his arms.*[2]

The human heart leans toward autonomous self-rule. We want to make our own rules, even redefining what good and evil mean (Gen. 3:5-7). This was the choice Adam and Eve made, and as their children we bear their likeness and share their corruption (Gen. 5:3).

What's so attractive about making our own rules?

Humanism disagrees. The *American Humanist Association* defines humanism as:

> *A progressive philosophy of life that, without theism and other supernatural beliefs, affirms our ability and responsibility to lead ethical lives of personal fulfillment that aspire to the greater good of humanity.*[3]

Humanism says God is no longer necessary to guide us in morality, help us understand what is ultimately good, or define what it means to be human. We are the masters of our own universe, shaping reality to our will, and defining these things ourselves.

Humanism crumbles under the weight of this task because it is fundamentally flawed as a worldview. Consider these four reasons humanism is a hopeless pursuit, based on the motivations of the human heart.

Reason 1: Humanism is proud.

The underlying motivation of pride is likely humanism's biggest flaw. While God "opposes the proud but shows favor to the humble" (1 Pet. 5:5), humanism embraces pride. Consider the following passage from the *Humanist Manifesto III*.

> *Knowledge of the world is derived by observation, experimentation, and rational analysis. ... We aspire to this vision with the informed conviction that humanity has the ability to progress toward its highest ideals. The responsibility for our lives and the kind of world in which we live is ours and ours alone.[4]*

These words show extreme optimism in human potential. They say we can progress without God, just with our own natural resources. This is not confidence but pride, similar to the attitude of the engineers who constructed the Tower of Babel:

> *Come, let us build ourselves a city, with a tower that reaches to the heavens, so that we may make a name for ourselves.*
> **GENESIS 11:4**

The humanist's belief that we alone are responsible for our lives and world is little different in concept from the builders' desire to make a name for themselves. Both attitudes are prideful because they suggest humanity can be great without God—an idea that is directly rejected throughout the Bible. In fact, the mindset that we can be the gods of our own existence is what led to Satan's rebellion (Isa. 14:12-14; Ezek. 28:17) and humanity's fall (Gen. 3:5).

Why are you sometimes tempted to believe you are the god of your own existence?

Read the following passages and list what they say about the possibility of achieving greatness apart from God.

> *"My thoughts are not your thoughts, neither are your ways my ways," declares the LORD.*
> *"As the heavens are higher than the earth, so are my ways higher than your ways and my thoughts than your thoughts."*
> **ISAIAH 55:8-9**

> *To those who by persistence in doing good seek glory, honor and immortality, he will give eternal life. But for those who are self-seeking and who reject the truth and follow evil, there will be wrath and anger.*
> **ROMANS 2:7-8**

If greatness apart from God is not possible, why is this something we sometimes want? When have you wanted to be great without God?

Reason 2: Humanism lacks moral humility.

As the apostle Paul explained, we each have God's moral law written on our hearts (Rom. 2:14-15). By contrast, the *American Humanist Association*'s motto is "Good without a God." They even believe each person has "inherent worth and dignity."[5] This is a valid ideal expressed in the Bible. However, humanism demonstrates its lack of moral humility in two ways.

1. Humanism fails to adequately account for the condition of the human heart. It does not acknowledge the fact that humans have a natural tendency toward evil, sin, and destruction. We are not upright moral beings. This fact is often challenged, but consider that the twentieth century was among the most violent in all of recorded history, with hundreds of millions of people murdered at the hands of oppressive government regimes. As genocide researchers have confirmed, a potential moral monster lurks inside each one of us. Here the Bible and human experience are in agreement with one another.

Read the following passages and list the ways they describe the condition of the human heart.

- **Psalm 51:5**

- **Jeremiah 17:9**

- **Romans 3:23-24**

In what ways do we resist the belief that we are sinful rebels? Can we really say someone is a great person? Why or why not?

2. Humanism makes a mistake in deriving objective moral values such as inherent worth and dignity from our human needs and desires. We cannot be the moral lawgivers who supply objective moral values, because we are immoral rebels who are unable to transcend (go beyond or surpass) ourselves or our sinful state.

Assuming that we can rise above ourselves by assigning a transcendent quality to our own needs, interests, and experiences is the height of arrogance. When we do this, we remake God in our own image, which the apostle Paul warned against in the strongest terms.

Read Romans 1:21-23,25, and 32.
What did the people not do in this passage? What was God's response?

Describe the exchange the people made. Why was this not a "good" trade?

Not only did the people live sinfully, they also _____ of those who did.

We cannot replace God in this way, because He is holy and we are not.

Ultimately, the standard of what is right and wrong is not determined by sinful human beings but a holy God. Why must we always consider how sin looks from His perspective?

Where in your life are you most tempted to choose your own perspective on sin over God's? What drives you to do this?

Followers of Jesus seek to avoid sin by knowing and obeying God's will. Read the following passage and consider what God's will is for your life.

Jesus replied: " 'Love the Lord your God with all your heart and with all your soul and with all your mind.' This is the first and greatest commandment. And the second is like it: 'Love your neighbor as yourself.' All the Law and the Prophets hang on these two commandments."
MATTHEW 22:37-40

RELATIVISM AND PERSONHOOD

Our second study picks up where the first study left off.

Reason 3: Humanism undermines personhood.

> **personhood:** a religious and philosophical term used to describe a person's status as one who holds human rights, feelings, ideas, and traits.

The *Humanist Manifesto III* makes clear that humanism is a work in progress, but human beings are still worthy of dignity and respect.

> *The lifestance [belief system] of Humanism—guided by reason, inspired by compassion, and informed by experience—encourages us to live life well and fully. It evolved through the ages and continues to develop through the efforts of thoughtful people who recognize that values and ideals, however carefully wrought, are subject to change as our knowledge and understandings advance. ... Humanists are concerned for the well being of all, are committed to diversity, and respect those of differing yet humane views. We work to uphold the equal enjoyment of human rights and civil liberties in an open, secular society and maintain it is a civic duty to participate in the democratic process.[6]*

Here is the problem: What happens when those who accept or sympathize with humanism change their minds and are no longer interested in being concerned with the wellbeing of others? Simply put: What happens when a revolution of ideas occurs and the outcome is not so positive?

For example, suppose someone takes to heart Richard Dawkins's claim that the universe has "no design, no purpose, no evil and no good,"[7] or experiences the same "epiphany" as atheist philosopher Joel Marks that "without God, there is no morality."[8] Given the hopeless condition of the human heart, what evil conduct might result from this?

Humanism that lacks a transcendent, value-giving authority can be easily toppled by a change of human will, because no one is ever right or wrong. Without God each of us is his or her own king or queen, and we step into the realm of the purely subjective, where phrases like "intrinsic value" and "right or wrong" have no real meaning.

God created all of us with objective purpose and meaning (Gen. 1:28–31). Why must we always determine our worth based on the objective standard of God's Word?

What happens when we find our sense of purpose and meaning in another source?

In a purely humanistic world, even the very concept of personhood can be lost. In Jesus' time, only a Roman citizen was considered a true person. David Bentley Hart noted that we now use the word *person* with "a splendidly indiscriminate generosity, applying it without hesitation to everyone, regardless of social station, race, or sex."[9] But this practice exists only because of the influence of Christianity.

If we abandon God, as humanism encourages, then there is no reason governments cannot become the dispensers of personhood once again, granting it to some and denying it to others. Indeed, this is America's own legal heritage as recently as 1856.[10]

Humanism not only makes morality relative, but also opens the door to making personhood relative. As Os Guinness explained:

> *Man made only in the image of Man loses his and*
> *her inviolability, for dignity that is self-created*
> *is weaker than dignity that is conferred. Mere*
> *existence does not add up to human dignity. ...*
> *Only if humans are made in the image of God—*
> *may they be physically and mentally handicapped,*
> *socially degraded or educationally deprived—can*
> *they always and irrevocably have a precious*
> *and inalienable dignity that none may abrogate*
> *or harm.*[11]

So, the only true humanism that objectively affirms human existence, dignity, and personhood is Christian humanism. The Bible reveals that these cherished values are not grounded in human agreement, reason, or experience (Rom. 12:2; 1 John 2:15-17) but in God Himself.

What does each of the following verses reveal about human equality, purpose, or meaning? How does each demonstrate that these ideas are rooted in God?

- **Equality and unity: Galatians 3:28; Philippians 2:3-7**

- **Dignity: Genesis 1:26-27; 9:6**

- **Purpose and meaning: Psalm 8:6-8**

- **Intentionality and design: Psalm 139:13-16**

Reason 4: Humanism misplaces its hope for the future.

When it comes to death, humanism puts on a brave face. As the *Humanist Manifesto III* remarks:

> *We accept our life as all and enough, distinguishing things as they are from things as we might wish or imagine them to be. ... We aim for our fullest possible development and animate our lives with a deep sense of purpose, finding wonder and awe in the joys and beauties of human existence, its challenges and tragedies, and even in the inevitability and finality of death.[12]*

Humanists cannot offer hope beyond the material world. The humanist's hope is really a futile attempt to reconstruct reality according to personal wishes. But saying something does not make it so. In reality, there is no "wonder and awe ... in the inevitability and finality of death" for the two following reasons.

1. Human death is the result of humankind's rebellion (Gen. 2:17; Rom. 5:12).

Read the following verses about death and fill in the blanks.

Romans 6:23; James 1:15 ⇨ _____ leads to death.

1 Corinthians 15:26 ⇨ At the end of time, when heaven is ushered in, the last enemy to be destroyed will be _____ itself.

2 Timothy 1:10 ⇨ _____ has destroyed death.

Revelation 1:18 ⇨ _____ holds the keys to death in His hands.

Revelation 20:14; 21:4 ⇨ Death will ultimately be thrown into the _____ and will be no more.

How many of your friends would recognize the link between sin and death? What dangers come from failing to recognize the cause of death?

Sin is both our enemy and God's enemy. Therefore, the apostle Paul dared to taunt death because of his victory through Christ:

> *When the perishable has been clothed with the imperishable, and the mortal with immortality, then the saying that is written will come true: "Death has been swallowed up in victory."*
> *"Where, O death, is your victory?*
> *Where, O death, is your sting?"*
> *The sting of death is sin, and the power of sin is the law. But thanks be to God! He gives us the victory through our Lord Jesus Christ.*
> **1 CORINTHIANS 15:54-57**

2. Death was never meant to be wonderful. Death is a punishment for sin and rebellion; however, for people who trust in Jesus Christ, death is anything but final. Because of Jesus' death and resurrection, death will not have the last word. Jesus taught that we are soul-ish beings—a functional unity of body and soul—not just material, biological machines (Matt. 10:28).

   How does it encourage you to know that Jesus, not death, has the last word on your eternity?

We are not headed for death and injustice but for greater and greater life. Not only has death been overcome, but we will also reign with God "for ever and ever" (Rev. 22:5) as "a royal priesthood" (1 Pet. 2:9). Professor Clay Jones summarized this truth well:

> God is giving us the kingdom and not just any kingdom, but the *kingdom*. And once Jesus comes, there will be no other. We get it all. ... He is giving us a controlling interest in part of heaven. He talks about ruling cities, He talks about true riches, He tells us to be faithful over things here. ... Truly. Big. Things. Come. We are going to reign over them, and we are going to do this with Jesus. That is God's plan for our lives, and it has always been the plan.[13]

That is the kind of eternity that deserves our "wonder and awe," one in which we can be "set free in [God's] universe, empowered to do what we want to do"[14] and were made to do.

Take a minute to read Psalm 118:9; 146:3; and Proverbs 27:1.

Some people claim it is possible to create heaven or a utopia here on earth apart from God. Why would it be a mistake to put our hope in a future utopia founded solely on human efforts?

Jesus conquered sin and death by enduring suffering. If Jesus overcame Satan and evil through suffering, should we expect that our path will be any different (Eph. 6:12)? Why or why not?

How does a humanistic worldview fail to offer hope during difficult situations?

How should this knowledge—along with the eternal glory of heaven that awaits us—help us endure suffering in this life?

How could you respond to your friend's humanistic claims about finding meaning, purpose, and morality apart from God?

WEEK 5

Hedonism

START

In your conversations this past week, you asked:

Would you mind if I explained the central message of Christianity to you?

Were people willing to hear the Christian message? If so, how did they respond?

What did people find new or surprising?

What questions did they have?

Were you personally encouraged or discouraged (or both) by this experience of sharing the Christian message? In what ways?

How would you change the way you share the Christian message next time?

THIS WEEK'S TOPIC

Hedonism is the view that life is all about happiness or pleasure. Imagine you had a machine that would give you any experience you wanted (maybe before long there will be such a machine!). You could choose to experience winning Olympic gold, falling in love, or making a great scientific discovery. Although in reality you would be floating in a tank of goo with electrodes hooked up to your brain, you would be experiencing total pleasure.[1]

Given the choice, would you preprogram your experiences and plug into this machine? Why or why not?

If pleasure was the only thing that mattered in life, of course we would want to plug into this experience machine and tell every person we know to do the same. But there's a difference between feeling something as if it's happening and actually having that experience. For example, we don't just want to feel loved; we want to be loved.

What are some experiences you've had that you immediately encouraged others to try? Why?

Hedonism is not what we truly want, but is all that is left when all the other "isms" have left us feeling empty. We shouldn't just care about feeling good on the inside—we should also care about truth and the influence our lives have on the world around us.

A lot of people say, "I don't need God; I'm happy as I am." What would you say in response?

Is pleasure a good thing? Do you think God wants us to be happy? Explain.

Hedonism fails, but God does not. He is with us until the very end, offering His hope. He wants us to respond with integrity, compassion, love, and justice. He wants us to love and serve others sacrificially, bringing not only pleasure to our lives, but also forgiveness, peace, purpose, hope—fullness of life in Him.

WATCH

Use this space to take notes as you watch the video for Week 5.

1. We so often settle for the cheap _____, instead of all that God is offering us.

2. Happiness is a very _____ and _____ thing.

3. Anything that _____ you and _____ you in life is a legitimate pleasure, so long as it does not violate your ultimate purpose in life.

4. You have to have rules that govern even _____, otherwise you violate the ultimate _____.

5. All _____ comes at a _____.

6. When you go about it the wrong way, you're like a person walking with _____ bones; when you're restored to God, you're a person walking with _____ bones.

7. This body is the _____ of the living God. If this body is the _____, then this body is _____.

8. We have to find our meaning as a _____ of _____.

9. In giving our _____ for others, we find true _____ in Jesus, and in His Father, and in the Holy Spirit.

10. The wrong kind of pleasure destroys the _____ of that pleasure.

WORDS TO KNOW

Hedonism: the view that life is all about happiness or pleasure
Pleasure: enjoying the feeling of having one's needs, desires, or wishes met
Happiness: the sensation of contentment and wellness; delight
Joy: a deep sense of satisfaction and content that comes from having a relationship with God and fulfilling our purpose in Him; includes celebration and enjoyment

Answers: 1. imitation; 2. fluctuating, fleeting; 3. refreshes, delights; 4. pleasure, purpose; 5. pleasure, cost; 6. broken, mended; 7. temple, temple, sacred; 8. child, God; 9. lives, pleasure; 10. chaser

DEBRIEF

Happiness and pleasure are good things, but when we make happiness and pleasure the highest forms of good, we risk missing out on the best God has for us.

If you had to choose one word or phrase to express what makes a good life, what would it be? Why?

In the video, Ravi pointed out that all pleasure comes at a cost. For the right kind of pleasure, we pay for it before we have enjoyed it. For the wrong kind of pleasure, we pay for it after we have enjoyed it.

What are some examples of these statements?

As a child, Vince's brother traveled for twenty-seven hours through flight delays to get to Disney World. After finally arriving in Florida, he looked at the revolving baggage-claim carousel, which to him looked like a ride, and exclaimed, "Thanks, Dad! I love Disney World!" He was too quick to settle for so much less than his father had in store for him.

The temptation of hedonism is also a problem in the church. Sometimes we settle for far less than God has for us.

In what ways do we tend to settle for cheap, temporary imitations rather than waiting for the fullness of what God desires for us?

How has hedonism failed you?

In what ways could advances in technology (for example, virtual reality, augmented reality, and artificial intelligence) intensify the temptation to choose pleasure over what is good and true in the years ahead?

Was Jesus a hedonist? In what ways does Jesus' life challenge a hedonistic perspective?

How is the life Jesus calls us to live different from hedonism?

PRAYER

- Read Psalm 16:11. God says we do not need to spend our time in an endless, exhausting pursuit of pleasure. He is the One who can fill us with joy, and that joy is found when we rest in His presence.

- Take a minute to sit in silence. Identify one specific way you have been living like a hedonist, chasing pleasure without considering the cost rather than counting the cost as a follower of Jesus Christ.

- Finish this week's session by reading Psalm 51:1-17 aloud together as a prayer of reliance on God's mercy and love and as an expression of desire to find joy in Him. Consider taking turns, allowing each student to read one verse.

BRINGING UP YOUR FAITH

Use the following questions to start a conversation with a non-believer this week.

The Bible tells us that prayer is "powerful and effective" (Jas. 5:16). It is challenging to reflect on whether we really believe that statement and whether our disciplines of prayer reflect this truth.

This week's focus is telling someone who is not a Christian you believe prayer makes a difference and that you would like to pray for them. To help you along in this conversation, begin by asking:

Would it be alright if I prayed for you?

If they answer "Yes" to your question, ask what current needs they might have. What are they currently hoping for or struggling with? Ask if you can pray for them during your conversation.

It is easy to promise to pray for people and then walk away from the conversation and forget that promise. Praying for them right then, in person, keeps us from that temptation.

Someone once said that there are two ways to choose a coat. You can check all of the dimensions of the coat, or you can try it on. Both ways are important. Many people are not even willing to consider the possibility of God unless they can see that the dimensions—the evidence of science, philosophy, and history—at least point in God's direction.

But ultimately, if someone wants to know God, there is no substitute for encountering Him directly. In His generosity, God has given us the gift of prayer so we can do just that. Experiencing prayer may be a key step for some people on their journey toward trusting God and being clothed in Christ.

After you have finished praying, ask your friend what he or she thought about the experience of prayer. Tell that person you will continue to pray for his or her requests.

JOURNAL

Use this page to reflect on your conversation.

Whom did you talk with? What was your overall experience with this conversation?

How willing was the person to have a conversation with you? What obstacles did you encounter?

What insights did you gain about communicating truth with gentleness and respect?

PLEASURE

Imagine talking to a friend who says, "Even if God exists, and He sets the rules about morality, why would I want to worship Him? Why would I want to spend eternity with someone so, well, boring? He cares only about rules. He's no fun and doesn't want us to have any fun either."

How would you respond?

GOD IS FOR PLEASURE

Christianity has an undeserved bad reputation when it comes to pleasure. Contrary to popular opinion, God is actually for pleasure. This statement may sound surprising, but it is true. The fact that God wants us to find pleasure in this life is an important but overlooked component of the gospel.

When are you tempted to view heaven or following God as something boring rather than a reward?

To our culture, the decision to trust Christ is a decision to renounce pleasure altogether, which makes spending eternity in heaven with God sound like a punishment rather than a reward. Consider the following examples.

- The Irish playwright George Bernard Shaw, who won the Nobel Prize in Literature in 1925, wrote, "Heaven, as conventionally conceived, is a place so inane, so dull, so useless, so miserable, that nobody has ever ventured to describe a whole day in heaven."[2]

- Actor Jack Nicholson admits, "I always said, 'Hey, you can have whatever rules you want—I'm going to have mine. I'll accept the guilt. I'll pay the check. I'll do the time.' "[3]

- Mark Twain's letter to his wife is remarkable: "I am plenty safe enough in his hands; I am not in any danger from that kind of a Deity. The one that I want to keep out of the reach of is the caricature of him which one finds in the Bible. We (that one and I) could never respect each other, never get along together. I have met his superior a hundred times—In fact I amount to that myself."[4]

These conclusions are unfortunate, because the same God who made "the heavens and the earth" (Gen. 1:1) also made delicious food, the sensation of jumping into cool water on a hot day, sunrises and sunsets—and He called them all good.

Heaven will be full of murderers (Moses), adulterers (David), terrorists (Paul), thieves (Luke 23:40-43), and prostitutes (Rahab) who repented of their sin and chose to enjoy an eternity of pleasure with God.

Scripture often describes our reunion with Jesus as a banquet (Isa. 25:6; Matt. 22:2; 25:1-10; Mark 14:25; Rev. 19:9) and a joyful party (Luke 15:11-32). Moreover, Jesus ate so often with sinners that the Pharisees accused Him of being "a glutton and a drunkard" (Matt. 11:19). That is not a God who forbids pleasure!

When have you seen examples of the world misunderstanding God's rules as forbidding fun?

UNDERSTANDING PLEASURE

In C. S. Lewis's classic work, *The Screwtape Letters,* a senior demon (Screwtape) wrote a series of letters to his nephew (Wormwood) to assist him in securing the damnation of a man known as "the Patient." God is referred to as "the Enemy". The following passage is telling:

> *Never forget that when we are dealing with any pleasure in its healthy and normal and satisfying form, we are, in a sense, on the Enemy's ground. I know we have won many a soul through pleasure. All the same, it is His invention, not ours. ... All we can do is encourage the humans to take the pleasures which our Enemy has produced, at times, or in ways, or in degrees, which He has forbidden.*[5]

Do you think of pleasure as being unchristian? Why is this not the case?

What is an example of a pleasure God has intended for our good that leads to sin when it becomes our ultimate goal?

Although God is for pleasure, He is opposed to the misuse of pleasure because of its negative effects. And that is the very risk of pleasure—its abuse. Because the human heart has a way of corrupting legitimate pleasures into illegitimate ones, it is critical to understand how to handle pleasure from a biblical perspective. We will look at three important principles for handling pleasure in a biblical way.

Principle 1: Only temporary pleasure is found in this world.

Read the following verses and fill in the details about Solomon's life.

1 Kings 4:23, ESV ⇨ Solomon's daily provision of meat included _____ cattle.

1 Kings 4:26 ⇨ Solomon owned _____ horses at a time when animals represented wealth.

1 Kings 4:32 ⇨ Solomon spoke _____ proverbs and composed _____ songs.

1 Kings 10:14 ⇨ Every year Solomon received _____ talents of gold (1 talent = 75 pounds).

1 Kings 11:3 ⇨ Solomon had _____ wives and _____ concubines.

Even by the most immoral of modern standards, Solomon had all this world can offer: feasting, sex, money, fame, power, security, and wisdom (1 Kings 4:31,34; 7:1; 10:21,23). Yet here is what he concluded after fully enjoying these earthly delights:

> *I denied myself nothing my eyes desired;*
> *I refused my heart no pleasure.*
> *My heart took delight in all my labor,*
> *and this was the reward for all my toil.*

Yet when I surveyed all that my hands had done
and what I had toiled to achieve,
everything was meaningless, a chasing after the
wind; nothing was gained under the sun.
ECCLESIASTES 2:10-11

It is important to understand that the phrase "under the sun" (v. 11) is a Hebraic expression for "without God." As Ravi has written, paraphrasing G. K. Chesterton, "Meaninglessness does not come from being weary of pain. Meaninglessness comes from being weary of pleasure."[6]

Solomon understood that no pleasure in this world is lasting, so an abundance of pleasure can lead to meaninglessness. The things of this world are not worth loving as God ought to be loved, because the world and its desires will pass away (1 John 2:15-17).

What does the world tend to pursue and view as lasting? How do Solomon's words challenge those ideas?

Os Guinness wrote, "An endless proliferation of trivial and unworthy choices is not freedom but slavery by another name. ... Freedom is not the permission to do what we like but the power to do what we should."[7]

Do you think this is an accurate definition of freedom? Why or why not?

What instances can you identify in which this truth was highlighted?

SURVIVING PLEASURE BEFORE ETERNITY

For this second study, we pick up where the first study ended.

Principle 2: Pleasure can be an idol that diminishes our relationship with God, derails our lives, and distracts from God's purposes.

Recall that this is precisely Screwtape's advice to Wormwood: "All we can do is encourage the humans to take the pleasures which [God] has produced, at times, or in ways, or in degrees, which He has forbidden." The dangers of abusing pleasure are numerous.

Read the following verses and identify some of the negative effects of abusing pleasure.

Spiritual / Luke 8:14

Financial / Proverbs 21:17

Prayer / James 4:3

Righteousness / 2 Timothy 3:4

Quality of life / 1 Timothy 6:9

Freedom / Titus 3:3

Ultimately, an unrighteous, sinful abuse of pleasure can lead to the heart spiritually "freezing," a depraved mind, rejection of legitimate authority, degradation of the body, and an act of divine judgment in which God gives the sinner over to his or her self-destruction (Rom. 1:21-32; 2 Pet. 2).

Once again, God is for pleasure, but He is opposed to the misuse of pleasure because of the dangers involved. Hedonism is a disease of the heart that requires a supernatural remedy (Ezek. 36:26). Even so, we have a significant part to play in our sanctification.

Exactly how does someone enjoy legitimate pleasures without allowing them to become traps, idols, or distractions? Enjoying legitimate pleasures within God's reasonable limits is a matter of wisdom, self-discipline, and at times supernatural assistance from the Holy Spirit. In this regard, the Bible offers five critical words of instruction.

1. **Feed yourself well.** The abuse of pleasure in this life can be avoided by storing what is good, noble, holy, worthwhile, and righteous in our hearts (Ps. 119:9-11; Matt. 15:18-20; Eph. 5:15-20).

2. **Practice self-control.** Pleasure must be handled in moderation (Prov. 25:16), and the temptation to abuse it must be mastered (Gen. 4:7; 1 Pet. 5:8-9). Godly leaders gladly choose to suffer along with the people of God rather than enjoy the fleeting pleasures of sin (2 Tim. 2:22).

3. **Pursue sexual purity.** Each of us should honor marriage and sexuality as God designed them. Sexual immorality and lust are the results of our fallen sinful nature and are therefore contrary to God's holiness (Rom. 13:13; 1 Cor. 6:9-20; Gal. 5:19-21; Eph. 5:3; Col. 3:5-6; 1 Thess. 4:3; 1 Tim. 1:9-10; Heb. 13:4).

4. **Delight in what is best.** Feed something and it will grow; starve something and it will die. The righteous who delight in God's Word will receive wisdom and prosper like a tree planted by streams of water (Ps. 1:1-3; 119:127-131).

5. **Understand the big picture.** Jesus calls His followers to sacrificial love rather than the evasion of pain or the exhausting pursuit of pleasure (Luke 9:23; John 15:20; Phil 1:29; 3:10-11).

Which of these instructions is the most difficult for you to follow? Why?

Read Philippians 4:8. Do you take Paul's advice when selecting movies or TV shows to watch, music to download, books to read, and other entertainment to enjoy? Why or why not?

How can the things you enjoy become a means for you to enjoy God?

Principle 3: Eternal and ultimately fulfilling pleasure is found in a relationship with God.

C. S. Lewis wrote:

> *Scripture and tradition habitually put the joys of*
> *heaven into the scale against the sufferings of earth,*
> *and no solution of the problem of pain that does not*
> *do so can be called a Christian one.*[8]

The joys of heaven and the pleasures that await us there are additional parts of the gospel that deserve significant attention.

In Week 1, we reflected on the meaning of life by asking: Why do we exist? Now that you have completed five weeks of Bible study, try to answer this question in just a few sentences.

The Westminster Shorter Catechism summarizes the meaning of life this way: "Man's chief end is to glorify God, and to enjoy him forever."[9] How does your answer compare?

The promises of Scripture reflect this purpose for humankind. Consider the following biblical teachings.

- God is the reward for a life of faith (Gen. 15:1).

- God will fill us with joy in His presence and eternal pleasures at His right hand (Ps. 16:11).

- Those who delight themselves in the Lord will receive the desires of their hearts (Ps. 37:4).

- Following God leads us to sacrificial love and service of others, which not only bring pleasure, but also bring fullness of life (John 10:10).

- God promises a hundred times as much future reward to people who make sacrifices for Him (Mark 10:29-30).

- Jesus gave up heavenly comfort and luxury to come to earth and live in human poverty so we could become rich (Rom. 8:17; 2 Cor. 8:9).

- Happiness is a gift of God, who fills our hearts with joy (Acts 14:17).

Philosopher Richard Swinburne wrote:

> *Friendship with God [is] of supreme value, for he is (by definition) perfectly good and, being (by definition) omnipotent and omniscient, will ever be able to hold our interest by showing us new facets of reality and above all his own nature.*[10]

In heaven we will enjoy God through our friendship with Him, and we will glorify God because of who He is and the wonder with which He will fill our imaginations for all eternity. That is the ultimate, everlasting pleasure!

What does it mean to say that heaven is primarily a person rather than a place?

Why should we not want heaven if God was not there?

How could you now respond to your friend's assertion that God is not for pleasure (p. 88)?

Conversations That Count

START

In your conversation last week, you were challenged to ask a non-believer:

Would it be alright if I prayed for you?

Was your friend open to being prayed for? What was his or her response to being prayed for?

What did you learn from this experience?

In what types of future situations could you offer to pray for people who are not Christians?

Continue to pray for your friend's requests and follow up with him or her about these concerns. God has heard your prayer and is at work.

THIS WEEK'S TOPIC

Jesus' final charge to His disciples was to go to all the nations, making disciples as they went (Matt. 28:19-20; Acts 1:8).

> *Go and make disciples of all nations, baptizing them in the name of the Father and of the Son and of the Holy Spirit, and teaching them to obey everything I have commanded you.*
> **MATTHEW 28:19-20**

Many Christians want to honor Jesus' final wishes by sharing the gospel with others, but find it intimidating and don't know where to start. Taking conversation seriously as a spiritual discipline and as a key aspect of Christian discipleship is a good place to start.

In all of the Gospels, we see that Jesus spent a lot of time talking with people, so it's not unreasonable to think He influenced people as much through His conversational ministry as through His preaching ministry. But it is surprising that growing as a conversationalist is rarely mentioned in discussions of what it means to follow Jesus.

Why do you think we don't put as much emphasis on developing as conversationalists as we put on other aspects of Christian discipleship?

One reason we often find it difficult to move conversations from small talk to talking about Jesus is that we spend so much of our conversational time just "talking small." Nothing is wrong with small talk, but Jesus always made the transition to deep, meaningful conversations. Like Him, we need to spend more of our time talking about meaningful topics, especially spiritual ones.

How can we develop the habit of spending more of our time in meaningful conversations?

What are some meaningful topics we could discuss that might lead to conversations about spiritual truth?

WATCH

Use this space to take notes as you watch the video for Week 6.

1. Jesus spent a lot of time in _____ with people.

2. Find something that person cares about. There's something they care about that you could _____ in.

3. If you are _____ of a subject, you will never enter a conversation with a hardened skeptic.

4. _____ is a great answer.

5. Be a better _____ _____ and be a better _____ to _____ .

6. If you're a _____ Christian, the question "How was your weekend?" is an absolute gift that we just pass up all the time.

7. A conversation is a means of _____ a _____ relationship.

8. _____ _____ is a good way to lead into opening the _____ of a person.

9. God will use what you _____ .

10. Conversations that _____ and invitations that _____ .

WORDS TO KNOW

Skeptic: someone who doubts things in general, or specifically doubts anything relating to religion

Trust: the ability to rely on the character of the person speaking, confidence in the truth of his or her claims

Answers: 1. conversations; 2. invest; 3. fearful; 4. "I don't know"; 5. question asker, responder, questions; 6. churchgoing; 7. establishing, trusted; 8. Asking questions, heart; 9. have; 10. count, matter

DISCUSS

God knew the best way to establish a relationship with humanity was to come to us and speak our language. Maybe you do this in some of your friendships or family relationships. For example, your dad enjoys baseball and you begin watching his favorite team to have something to talk about with him, some way to connect with him.

What are some ways you can invest in the interests of people with whom you would like to share the gospel?

Be ready to ask good questions. Jesus asked a lot of good questions—one estimate is that 307 of them are recorded in the New Testament. But our most common questions tend to lack creativity: "How was your weekend?" "Did you have a good summer?" "How's it going?" "How's school?" These questions can be (and usually are) answered in three words or less, without any meaningful information being shared.

Read over the "Questions That Count" at the end of this session. What questions do you like? What do you like about them?

What are some other meaningful questions you could add to this list?

Be ready to give good responses. When Jesus responded to a question, He did so with discernment and purpose: "Why do you call me good?" (Mark 10:18); "Give back to Caesar what is Caesar's, and to God what is God's" (Matt. 22:21); and "Let any one of you who is without sin be the first to throw a stone" (John 8:7).

Maybe one reason Jesus was able to respond with such wisdom and intentionality is that He prayed about the questions and challenges He saw coming. We also know many of the questions we are asked regularly or will be asked in certain situations. Will we take time to be prepared to respond in meaningful ways that can lead to conversations that count?

What questions do people often ask you that you respond to in a routine way?

How could we respond to those questions in creative ways that could lead to meaningful conversations?

When we respond meaningfully to everyday questions, we build deeper relationships and create a space where people will be more likely to ask us questions about our faith. As we trust God for deeper conversations in our daily lives and people begin to ask difficult questions, it is important to remember that "I don't know" is a valid answer. People do not want to join a community of know-it-alls. People want to join a community that cares enough to take their questions seriously, do some research, and come back with a thoughtful response and an invitation to continue the conversation.

Be invitational. People don't usually show up to a party if they did not receive an invitation. Moreover, receiving an invitation to a party is a gift, even if the person who is invited decides that he or she is unable to attend.

Why do you think we tend to be hesitant about inviting people into the Christian life—to the party God is throwing? Will you accept God's invitation to be involved in inviting people into a relationship with Him?

PRAYER

- Read Romans 1:16. Lead your group in a time of silent prayer asking God to bring to mind someone to whom He wants you to extend His invitation to know and follow Him.

- Commit to pray daily during the coming week for the people in your group and for God to bless the invitations they will offer. Follow up next week to learn how things have gone, to encourage one another, and to find out how you can continue to pray. May God grant us the faith and courage we need for the words of Romans 1:16 to be true of us.

BRINGING UP YOUR FAITH

Use the following questions to start a conversation with a non-believer this week.

We hope you have been encouraged and challenged by these weekly tips for bringing up your faith, and we hope you will make them a part of your everyday life.

These are practical ways we can love people well by interacting with them in meaningful ways. For example, if you know you will see someone tomorrow, ask God tonight if there is a question He wants you to ask them or if there is a response He wants you to give to a question they always ask you.

During the next week ask someone who is not a Christian:

What keeps you from giving your life to Jesus?

If they do not identify a significant obstacle, ask if they want to pray to ask God to forgive their sins and to tell Him they want to follow Him.

If people aren't ready to take this step, ask if they would be willing to pray something like this:

God, I'm not sure if You are there, but if You are, I would really like to know it. If You show Yourself to me, I will put my trust in You.

We have seen God honor this very powerful prayer countless times.

If we all commit to having this conversation, by this time next week we believe we will have new brothers and sisters in Christ and that eternal destinies will have been transformed!

We do not know which of our invitations will be accepted, but there is power in community. If we each commit to offer one invitation, we will help motivate one another. Regardless of which invitations are accepted, we all will have had the amazing privilege and eternal joy of participating in building God's kingdom.

JOURNAL

Use this page to reflect on your conversation.

Whom did you talk with? What was your overall experience with this conversation?

How willing was the person to have a conversation with you? What obstacles did you encounter?

What insights did you gain about communicating truth with gentleness and respect?

RELATIONAL NETWORKS

LIVING AS INSIDERS

Each of us is one of God's insiders among our family members, friends, neighbors, teammates, and social networks. As insiders, we play an indispensable role in working out God's purposes, because each of us has inside access to a unique set of relationships through which the gospel can organically move and advance.[1]

Sound too easy? Certainly, an effective insider ministry takes time and intentionality. Jesus did not just eat and drink with sinners and tax collectors (Matt. 11:19); He lingered with them, spending quality time serving and ministering to them. And an insider must do the same. These people are not "projects" or strangers but friends, relatives, and classmates who already have a meaningful presence in our lives.

The gospel spreads most naturally through relational networks; therefore, a ministry field surrounds each one of us.

Read Mark 5:1-20 to see how Jesus provided an example of this during His earthly ministry.

> As Jesus was getting into the boat, the man who had been demon-possessed begged to go with him. Jesus did not let him, but said, "Go home to your own people and tell them how much the Lord has done for you, and how he has had mercy on you." So the man went away and began to tell in the Decapolis how much Jesus had done for him. And all the people were amazed.
> **MARK 5:18-20**

The man had an _____ _____ (v. 2). What did Jesus do to help him?

What was the crowd's reaction to Jesus helping the man? What was the man's reaction?

List Jesus' instructions to the man in this passage. How was the man an insider and to whom?

Jesus sent the man to his "own people" to "tell them how much the Lord" had done for him (v. 19). In other words, Jesus sent the man back to the place where he was an insider. There, the man would already be known, and the testimony of his life-changing encounter with Jesus might be more readily accepted.

List some places where you are an insider.

Who in those places most needs to hear about Jesus? Pause for a moment to pray for them.

COME AND SEE

John wrote about Jesus gathering His first disciples (1:35-50). These men did not know much about Jesus at the time, but they perceived enough to take an interest in Him, and over time they began to follow Him. Let's consider what we can learn about our own witness for Jesus.[2]

Read John 1:35–50. Andrew, Simon, Philip, and Nathanael were all introduced to Jesus in this passage. What were their attitudes toward Jesus before meeting Him? What was each man's initial understanding of Jesus?

How was each man introduced to Jesus? What similarities and differences did you see?

What was each man's reaction to hearing about Jesus? How did each man respond to meeting Jesus and hearing His response to them? What similarities and differences did you see?

Think back to the time someone first invited you to follow Jesus. Who were the key people who introduced you to Jesus? What did they do? What did they say, and how did they say it?

What was your initial reaction and response to their invitation?

We can make four key observations from this account in which Andrew, Simon, Philip, and Nathanael were introduced to Jesus.

1. **Everyone has a different starting point.** Before being introduced to Jesus, each person had a different attitude, knowledge base, and level of interest. In terms of attitude, Nathanael was clearly skeptical, and Simon may have been as well. In contrast, both Andrew and Philip were quite enthusiastic. In terms of knowledge, Andrew received information about Jesus from John the Baptist, and both Philip and Nathanael seemed to have some knowledge of the Torah.

2. **Personal introductions are important.** Four of the five men in this passage (one is unnamed) were introduced to Jesus by someone else through testimony, invitation, or persuasion. Only Philip was directly called by Jesus.

3. **We must invite others to come and see Jesus.** Both Andrew and Philip went and told others (Simon and Nathanael, respectively) about Jesus and invited them to "come and see" (v. 46). Even though we cannot physically do this today, we can introduce others to Jesus through His bride—the church—or through Jesus' life and teaching in the Bible (Heb. 4:12).

4. **The process can take time.** Even though Simon was introduced to Jesus by his brother Andrew, neither he nor Andrew left everything and followed Jesus until sometime later (Matt. 4:18-20). Jesus taught that His disciples must count the cost of following Him (Luke 14:25-33), and this process can take months, years, or even a lifetime.

   Think of someone in your life who does not know Jesus. What can you do to introduce that person to Jesus? How would you go about it?

   What questions might you ask to start a conversation that leads to Christ?

ENGAGING WITH OTHERS

From an evangelistic standpoint perhaps no conversation recorded in the Bible teaches us more about conversations that count than Jesus' conversation with a Samaritan woman recorded in John 4:3-26,39-42. We will examine this passage in detail, analyzing it one segment at a time in order to draw out a number of important evangelistic principles.

Principle 1: Be willing to break through social and cultural barriers.

> *[Jesus] left Judea and went back once more to Galilee. Now he had to go through Samaria. So he came to a town in Samaria called Sychar, near the plot of ground Jacob had given to his son Joseph. Jacob's well was there, and Jesus, tired as he was from the journey, sat down by the well. It was about noon. When a Samaritan woman came to draw water, Jesus said to her, "Will you give me a drink?" (His disciples had gone into the town to buy food.) The Samaritan woman said to him, "You are a Jew and I am a Samaritan woman. How can you ask me for a drink?" (For Jews do not associate with Samaritans.)*
> **JOHN 4:3-9**

There is some debate about whether Jesus actually "had" to go through Samaria (v. 4). The region of Samaria was located between Judea in the south and Galilee in the north. While going through Samaria was the quickest route, some Jews preferred to take the long way back to Galilee to avoid Samaria altogether.

Many Jews believed Samaritans to be an unclean "half-breed" because of their intermarriage with Assyrians during the exile.[3] Clearly, Jesus did not care for this prejudice and willingly talked with those whom his culture looked down on.

The woman herself was likely a social outcast, as evidenced by the fact that she came to the well alone at noon.[4] Jesus had every cultural reason to overlook this woman because of her ethnic identity, gender, and social status. But Jesus didn't overlook the *imago Dei*—the image of God—each person bears, and neither should we.

What social and cultural barriers are you afraid to cross, even to share the gospel?

Principle 2: Generate curiosity about Jesus. Having earned trust by violating social taboos, Jesus next made an unusual statement.

> *Jesus answered her, "If you knew the gift of God and who it is that asks you for a drink, you would have asked him and he would have given you living water." "Sir," the woman said, "you have nothing to draw with and the well is deep. Where can you get this living water? Are you greater than our father Jacob, who gave us the well and drank from it himself, as did also his sons and his livestock?"*
> **JOHN 4:10-12**

Jesus used the well to start a conversation about Himself. By making the claim about living water, Jesus piqued the woman's curiosity. Even though the woman may not have believed Jesus right away, He certainly had her attention.

What is an example of something in our culture that you can use to begin a conversation about Jesus?

Principle 3: Present the gospel. The "living water" (v. 10) Jesus offered didn't come from a well in the ground; Jesus was referring to the Holy Spirit, who gives eternal life (John 7:38-39), and He was far greater than the patriarchs (Heb. 3:3).

> *Jesus answered, "Everyone who drinks this water will be thirsty again, but whoever drinks the water I give them will never thirst. Indeed, the water I give them will become in them a spring of water welling up to eternal life." The woman said to him, "Sir, give me this water so that I won't get thirsty and have to keep coming here to draw water."*
> **JOHN 4:13-15**

Jesus' words echo Old Testament promises (Isa. 12:3; 44:3; 49:10; 55:1-5; Jer. 2:13; Zech. 14:8). The woman was beginning to understand what Jesus was saying and the hope He offered.

Refer to your answer to the previous question. How can you move from that conversation starting point to the gospel?

Principle 4: Highlight the need for the gospel.

> *He told her, "Go, call your husband and come back."*
> *"I have no husband," she replied. Jesus said to her,*
> *"You are right when you say you have no husband.*
> *The fact is, you have had five husbands, and the*
> *man you now have is not your husband. What you*
> *have just said is quite true."*
> **JOHN 4:16-18**

Jesus addressed the Samaritan woman's emotional needs for security and significance, as He addressed her sin. Although these needs had driven her to a life of sexual immorality, Jesus invited her to come as she was so that God could satisfy the thirsts of her heart and soul.

What big questions are people asking that Jesus can answer? How do these questions help point the way to Jesus?

Principle 5: When objections arise, stay focused on what matters.

> *"Sir," the woman said, "I can see that you are a*
> *prophet. Our ancestors worshiped on this mountain*
> *[Mount Gerizim], but you Jews claim that the place*
> *where we must worship is in Jerusalem." "Woman,"*
> *Jesus replied, "believe me, a time is coming when*
> *you will worship the Father neither on this mountain*
> *nor in Jerusalem. You Samaritans worship what*
> *you do not know; we worship what we do know,*
> *for salvation is from the Jews. Yet a time is coming*
> *and has now come when the true worshipers will*

*worship the Father in the Spirit and in truth, for they
are the kind of worshipers the Father seeks. God is
spirit, and his worshipers must worship in the Spirit
and in truth." The woman said, "I know that Messiah"
(called Christ) "is coming. When he comes, he will
explain everything to us." Then Jesus declared, "I,
the one speaking to you—I am he."*

JOHN 4:19-26

Jesus had tapped into an area of insecurity, a deep wound of guilt and hurt. The Samaritan woman naturally attempted to move Him away from this area of her life.

How can we listen thoughtfully and attentively to objections without allowing ourselves to get sidetracked?

Jesus focused on three truths that really mattered:

God's Word. Because Samaritans rejected much of the Old Testament, they stood outside the stream of God's saving revelation. Jesus addressed the fact that the Samaritans worshiped a God they did not fully know. The integrity and authority of Scripture is never a place of compromise.

Relationship with God. Sidestepping the theological debate about the relative merits of Jerusalem and Mount Gerizim, Jesus instead focused on the person of God rather than a place. What mattered was not where someone worshiped but whom.

The identity of Jesus. Before His trial, this was Jesus' only open declaration that He was the Messiah. The full disclosure of who Jesus is—Messiah, Son of God, King, Prophet, Great High Priest—can be powerful when a heart is open to the truth. This one conversation immediately changed life and eternity for this woman and those she knew:

*Many of the Samaritans from that town believed in
[Jesus] because of the woman's testimony, "He told
me everything I ever did." So when the Samaritans
came to him, they urged him to stay with them, and
he stayed two days. And because of his words many
more became believers.*

JOHN 4:39-41

Later the ministry begun there paved the way for successful evangelism by Philip (Acts 8:4-13) and Peter and John (vv. 14-25).

In their book *I Once Was Lost* authors Don Everts and Doug Schaupp outline five thresholds that people generally pass through on their journeys to becoming followers of Jesus:

---

1. **Trusting a Christian**
2. **Becoming curious about Jesus**
3. **Opening up to change**
4. **Seeking God**
5. **Entering the kingdom**[5]

Consider these thresholds as you answer the following questions.

Think of the social networks in which you are an insider. At which of the five thresholds would you place each of the main people in your life?

How can you use questions and stories in ways that provoke curiosity about Jesus?

Why might you need to gently but boldly call people out of fear and complacency?

Paul instructs us to be both wise and gracious (Col. 4:5-6). What does it mean for speech to be gracious? What does it mean for our words to be seasoned with salt?

How does this manner of speech affect the way you answer each person?

QUESTIONS THAT COUNT

- What was the best part of your week? What was the worst part of your week?

- What has been on your mind most recently?

- When was the happiest time in your life? Why?

- What are you good at?

- What are your dreams for the future?

- If money was not an issue and you could do anything you wanted, what would you do? Why?

- What were you like as a child? What ways are you different now?

- What is your best childhood memory?

- What family member are you most alike? What family member are you most different from? In what ways?

- To which family member are you closest? Are you close to your other family members?

- Who is your best friend, and what is his or her best quality?

- How would your best friends describe you?

- Who has had the most significant influence on your life? Why?

- What would you change about yourself if you could change one thing?

- Have you grown up in a religious home? Would you raise your children the same way? Why or why not?

- What do you find most frustrating about religion?

- If you could make one law, what would it be? If you could break one law, what would it be?

- In one word, what do you think is the most important trait in a leader?

- What causes 80 percent of your stress?

- What experiences have you had that made you think God might exist?

OUR QUESTIONS

Use this page to record big questions you may have about God, faith, or life.

Leader Guide

We're so excited for you to join us as we journey through *Jesus Among Secular Gods*! This study will not only teach students how to answer tough questions from nonbelievers, but will also address some of their own tough questions. Here are some things you need to know to be an effective leader.

FORMAT

OPEN

In the first session, open by introducing the main ideas of the study. In the following sessions, you will begin by discussing the previous week's Bringing Up Your Faith. Then, introduce the current week's topic by using the This Week's Topic section. Prompts and discussion questions are provided for both sections.

As an option, bonus videos will be provided for each session. These include interviews about faith with Vince Vitale and students from Princeton University. Each video clip is between 1 and 5 minutes, and we provide discussion questions to help students further engage with what they've seen and heard. These clips are also a great option for midweek or Sunday night studies.

WATCH

Watch the videos for the session together. Keep in mind that these are difficult topics, so the videos are between 15 to 25 minutes each. This page includes space for students to take notes as they watch the video. It also identifies key terms and definitions referenced in the session.

DEBRIEF

This time provides the opportunity for your group to talk about what they learned during the week and debrief what they learned in the video teaching. Each guide begins with questions designed to help students think through the themes their study covers throughout the week.

CLOSE

You will be given reminders and words of encouragement to share with your group and/or prayer prompts to close your session.

WEEK 1

OPEN

- Give each student a *Jesus Among Secular Gods* book, and use the Promo clip to introduce the study.
- Use the Start section (p. 9) to talk about some of life's biggest questions and introduce students to our need to constantly be prepared to answer questions about our faith.
- Introduce students to the topic of study for the week by guiding them through This Week's Topic (p. 10).

WATCH

- View the video for Week 1.
- Instruct students to follow the guide on page 11 and to take note of the key terms and definitions listed at the bottom of the page.

DEBRIEF

- Review the video by guiding students through the questions and prompts on pages 12-13.
- Optional: If time allows, choose one of the bonus video clips provided for this session. Place students in smaller groups and allow them to answer the following discussion questions together. *(Tip: You may want to choose just one key question if you're pushed for time.)*

- *What If?* Students share about the hope our faith in God provides
  1. Where would you find your hope if God didn't exist?
  2. When have you been tempted to place your hope in your accomplishments, family, friends, or status?
  3. How does the fear of failure affect the way you live? How do you think that would change if running to God were not an option?
  4. How does God's presence in your life affect the way you respond in difficult circumstances?
  5. Where has God met you and provided hope when things seemed hopeless?

- *Tough Questions* Students share about questions they have wrestled with on their own, as well as how to respond when nonbelievers challenge their faith.
  1. What challenges or questions have you had to wrestle with as you seek to grow in your relationship with God?
  2. When have you struggled with "just going through the motions"? How do you think this affects the way you respond when your faith is challenged?
  3. How have difficult conversations with nonbelievers strengthened your faith?

4. Are you generally willing to ask tough questions, despite others' reactions? Or are you tempted to stay quiet, fearing people will label you as a doubter, or worse? Explain.

5. What can we do to create an environment where tough questions can be asked? Why is this so important?

- *Wrecked* Students share how the world's standards drain us, while Christ frees us.

  1. Do you think it's more difficult to believe in God than not believe in God? Why or why not?

  2. What are some questions you're afraid of being asked by nonbelievers?

  3. What can you do when you're faced with questions you feel unprepared to answer?

  4. Where else are you sometimes tempted to turn for affirmation or fulfillment?

  5. What do you think it means to "be wrecked by the standards of the world around you"? When have you experienced this?

WEEKLY CHALLENGE

- Introduce the question and goal for Bringing up Your Faith on page 14 by explaining that the challenge will help students to practice what they are learning and start conversations with nonbelievers.
- Tell students that setting conversational goals in the context of community and encouraging one another in those goals can make a huge difference in the faithfulness and effectiveness of our attempts to share Christ with others.
- The goal this week is to ask two questions and listen well to the answers. These questions are meant to lead you into conversations about faith. This week's questions are:
  - What is your biggest objection to Christianity?
  - What do you think it would take for you to change your mind about God and become a Christian?

CLOSE

- Remind students to complete the On Your Own section on pages 14-25. This section includes: a weekly challenge called Bringing up Your Faith (p. 14), journal questions to help students respond to the weekly challenge (p. 15), and two Personal Study sections (pp. 16-25).
- Close your group time in prayer, using the prompts in the Prayer section on page 13 to pray specifically over issues you've touched on this week as you studied what it means to be prepared to share your faith at all times, in all circumstances.

WEEK 2

OPEN
- Use the Start section (p. 27) to discuss last week's challenge in Bringing up Your Faith (p. 14).
- Introduce students to the topic of study for the week, Atheism and Scientism, by guiding them through This Week's Topic (p. 28).

WATCH
- View the video for Week 2.
- Instruct students to follow the guide on page 29 and to take note of the key terms and definitions listed at the bottom of the page.

DEBRIEF
- Review the video by guiding students through the questions and prompts on pages 30-31.
- Optional: If time allows, show the bonus video clip provided for this session. Place students in smaller groups and allow them to answer the following discussion questions together. *(Tip: You may want to choose just one key question if you're pushed for time.)*

  - ***The Attractiveness of Atheism*** Students share what they believe atheists find attractive about the idea that there is no God.
    1. What role does pride play in choosing to believe or not believe in God?
    2. What's attractive about living for yourself? What changes when you live for God?
    3. Why is it sometimes difficult to believe in God while not knowing everything about Him?

WEEKLY CHALLENGE
- Introduce the question and goal for Bringing up Your Faith on page 32.
- Encourage students to give time for people to answer their questions, and remind them that being willing to listen well is key.
- This week's question is: Have you ever experienced something in your life that made you think there might be a God?

CLOSE
- Remind students to complete the On Your Own section on pages 32-43. This section includes: a weekly challenge called Bringing up Your Faith (p. 32), journal questions to help students respond to the weekly challenge (p. 33), and two Personal Study sections (pp. 34-43).
- Close your group time in prayer, using the prompts in the Prayer section on page 31 to pray specifically over issues you've touched on this week as you studied atheism and scientism.

WEEK 3

OPEN
- Use the Start section (p. 45) to discuss last week's challenge in Bringing up Your Faith (p. 32).
- Introduce students to the topic of study for the week, Pluralism, by guiding them through This Week's Topic (p. 46).

WATCH
- View the video for Week 3.
- Instruct students to follow the guide on page 47 and to take note of the key terms and definitions listed at the bottom of the page.

DEBRIEF
- Review the video by guiding students through the questions and prompts on pages 48-49.
- Optional: If time allows, choose one of the bonus video clips provided for this session. Place students in smaller groups and allow them to answer the following discussion questions together. *(Tip: You may want to choose just one key question if you're pushed for time.)*

  - **Naturally Offensive** Students share why the idea that all of humankind is sinful is naturally offensive, especially to non-Christians.
    1. When have you seen non-Christians become offended by interactions with Christians? What caused this to happen? How did the interaction end?
    2. Why do you think it's "naturally offensive" to be told that all of humankind in sinful?
    3. How can you graciously share with others the need to deal with their sin problem?
    4. When are you tempted to convince others that they are wrong so that you can then show them the right way?

  - **The Grace Aspect** Students share what they believe to be the key difference between Christianity and other religions—grace.
    1. What other religions have you heard of or studied?
    2. What are some similarities among those religions? Differences?
    3. According to the video, what is so different about Christianity compared to those religions?

  - **God-centered or Self-centered?** Students share about the differences in living a life that is God-centered and living a life that is self-centered.
    1. What's so difficult about only being able to understand God to a certain extent?
    2. How have you responded to "the glimpse" of God you have received?

3. Compare and contrast how your life is different when it is God-centered and when it is self-centered or world-centered.
4. Do you struggle with not having all the answers when it comes to life and God? Why or why not?

WEEKLY CHALLENGE
- Introduce the question and goal for Bringing up Your Faith on page 50.
- This week's question is: If God exists, what do you think He thinks of you?
- Explain the following to students.
  - This question can often expose that the God someone is rejecting is not the God of the Christian faith.
  - Some people may respond by saying they think God would be indifferent toward them.
  - Other people may respond by talking about what God would think of the way they have recently behaved. Be aware that there may be truth in this second response, but the question is not about what God thinks of their behavior but, more specifically, what God thinks of them.

CLOSE
- Remind students to complete the On Your Own section on pages 50-61. This section includes: a weekly challenge called Bringing up Your Faith (p. 50), journal questions to help students respond to the weekly challenge (p. 51), and two Personal Study sections (pp. 52-61).
- Close your group time in prayer, using the prompts in the Prayer section on page 49 to pray specifically over issues you've touched on this week as you studied pluralism.

WEEK 4

OPEN
- Use the Start section (p. 63) to discuss last week's challenge in Bringing up Your Faith (p. 50).
- Introduce students to the topic of study for the week, Humanism and Relativism, by guiding them through This Week's Topic (p. 64).

WATCH
- View the video for Week 4.
- Instruct students to follow the guide on page 65 and to take note of the key terms and definitions listed at the bottom of the page.

DEBRIEF
- Review the video by guiding students through the questions and prompts on pages 66-67.

- Optional: If time allows, choose one of the bonus video clips provided for this session. Place students in smaller groups and allow them to answer the following discussion questions together. *(Tip: You may want to choose just one key question if you're pushed for time.)*

  - *Control* A student shares about the truth of control and who really has the power to direct our lives.
    1. Do you like to be in control? Why or why not?
    2. Who else in your life tries to make decisions about your life for you? How do you respond when that happens?
    3. When are you tempted to think you can make the best decisions in life?
    4. Do you think what you want to do is always in your best interest? Why or why not?
    5. What happens when you realize you're not in control?

  - *The Intolerance of Tolerance* Students share about the devastating consequences of tolerance.
    1. What do you normally think of when you hear the word *tolerance*?
    2. In what ways does tolerance seem to shame people who hold views that go against popular opinion?
    3. How have you seen the tolerance culture be intolerant?
    4. How does the tolerance culture affect the way you share (or choose not to share) your views?

WEEKLY CHALLENGE
- Introduce the question and goal for Bringing up Your Faith on page 68.
- This week's question is: Would you mind if I explained the central message of Christianity to you?
- Tip: Write the Christian message in your own words, and then read it together with students.

CLOSE
- Remind students to complete the On Your Own section on pages 68-79. This section includes: a weekly challenge called Bringing up Your Faith (p. 68), journal questions to help students respond to the weekly challenge (p. 69), and two Personal Study sections (pp. 70-79).
- Close your group time in prayer, using the prompts in the Prayer section on page 67 to pray specifically over issues you've touched on this week as you studied Humanism and Relativism.

WEEK 5

OPEN
- Use the Start section (p. 81) to discuss last week's challenge in Bringing up Your Faith (p. 68).
- Introduce students to the topic of study for the week, Hedonism, by guiding them through This Week's Topic (p. 82).

WATCH
- View the video for Week 5.
- Instruct students to follow the guide on page 83 and to take note of the key terms and definitions listed at the bottom of the page.

DEBRIEF
- Review the video by guiding students through the questions and prompts on pages 84-85.
- Optional: If time allows, choose one of the bonus video clips provided for this session. Place students in smaller groups and allow them to answer the following discussion questions together. *(Tip: You may want to choose just one key question if you're pushed for time.)*

  - ***All About Happiness*** Students share how true happiness is found in God and the promises He has made.
    1. Life is all about happiness. True or false? Explain.
    2. How do past difficulties increase your joy in the present?
    3. What does it mean to be happy in God?
    4. What are some steps you can take this week to be happy in Him?

  - ***Was Jesus' Life "Happy"?*** Students describe the difference between happiness and joy, and how Jesus' example shows that not all of life is "happy."

    1. How does the world define happiness? How do you define happiness?
    2. How would you describe Jesus' life before He came to earth? What about while He was on earth?
    3. When you think about eternity, where does our happiness lie? Where are we ultimately headed?
    4. What's the difference between happiness and joy?

  - ***Impossible Happiness*** A student shares about the belief that people cannot be truly happy without God.
    1. What do you say to someone who says, "I am happy as I am"?
    2. Do you tend to believe people who claim to be happy without God? Why or why not?

3. What types of struggles do you think people are most likely to hide? Explain.

4. How would you describe your happiness in God to a non-believer?

WEEKLY CHALLENGE

- Introduce the question and goal for Bringing up Your Faith on page 86.
- This week's question is: Would it be alright if I prayed for you?
- Share with students that some people might say "no." In this case, students should continue to pray for that person on their own time. However, in most cases, people generally do not refuse prayer.
- Tell students that, after they have finished praying, they should ask people what they thought about the experience of prayer. Then, instruct students to tell the people they talked with that they will continue to pray for those requests.

CLOSE

- Remind students to complete the On Your Own section on pages 86-95. This section includes: a weekly challenge called Bringing up Your Faith (p. 86), journal questions to help students respond to the weekly challenge (p. 87), and two Personal Study sections (pp. 88-95).
- Close your group time in prayer, using the prompts in the Prayer section on page 85 to pray specifically over issues you've touched on this week as you studied Hedonism.

WEEK 6

OPEN

- Use the Start section (p. 97) to discuss last week's challenge in Bringing up Your Faith (p. 86).
- Introduce students to the topic of study for the week, Conversations That Count, by guiding them through This Week's Topic (p. 98).

WATCH

- View the video for Week 6.
- Instruct students to follow the guide on page 99 and to take note of the key terms and definitions listed at the bottom of the page.

DEBRIEF

- Review the video by guiding students through the questions and prompts on pages 100-101.
- Optional: If time allows, choose one of the bonus video clips provided for this session. Place students in smaller groups and allow them to answer the

following discussion questions together. *(Tip: You may want to choose just one key question if you're pushed for time.)*

- ***Bringing Up Your Faith*** Students share ways to bring up their faith naturally in relationships they already have.
  1. Where do you find it most difficult to share your faith? Where is it easy to share your faith?
  2. What are some ways you have shared your faith? Which do you think was most successful? Why?
  3. How does it affect you to know God did not call you to be comfortable?
  4. How might it grow your faith if you share the gospel, even when it isn't comfortable or cool?

- ***The Bible "Plus"*** Students share why keeping Scripture in context is so important when sharing their faith.
  1. What are some difficult questions people have asked you when it comes to your faith?
  2. How can these questions and conversations help you develop deeper relationships with those around you as you seek to share the gospel with them?
  3. When can it be tempting to take Scripture out of context when trying to answer a question in a way that will satisfy the questioner?
  4. How can we guard against using "the Bible plus..." in these conversations?

- ***When Questions Distract*** A student shares questions that may be uncomfortable or difficult to answer.
  1. What questions would you be least confident answering? Which would you be most confident answering?
  2. How do these questions sometimes distract from the main points of God's love for us, who Jesus is, and what He did for us?
  3. What are some ways we can redirect those questions to God?
  4. How can you fight the fear that you don't have the authority to answer tough questions, and what can you do when you don't know the answer?

WEEKLY CHALLENGE
- Introduce the question and goal for Bringing up Your Faith on page 102.
- This week's question is: What keeps you from giving your life to Jesus?
- Despite the fact that this is the last week of the study, remind students that their conversations can continue. Let students know you are available for questions they might have.

- Encourage students to begin new conversations as well. Remind them that this process can be repeated with new people, even while other conversations are ongoing.

CLOSE
- Remind students to complete the On Your Own section on pages 102-111. This section includes: a weekly challenge called Bringing up Your Faith (p. 102), journal questions to help students respond to the weekly challenge (p. 103), and two Personal Study sections (pp. 104-111).
- Allow students time to look over the Questions That Count on page 112. If time allows, discuss the questions students most commonly admit having and list them in the Our Questions section (p 113).
- Close your group time in prayer, using the prompts in the Prayer section on page 101 to pray specifically over issues you've touched on this week as you studied Conversations.

SOURCES

Week 1

1. Richard Dawkins, "The 'know-nothings', the 'know-alls', and the 'no contests', " *The Nullifidian*, December 1994.
2. Richard Dawkins, "Is Science a Religion?," *The Humanist*, January/February 1997, http://employees.oneonta.edu/blechmjb/jbpages/m205/Richard%20Dawkins%20Is%20Science%20A%20Religion.htm.
3. John C. Lennox, *God's Undertaker: Has Science Buried God?* (Oxford: Lion Books, 2009), 16.
4. Ibid.
5. Merriam-Webster Dictionary, s.v. "argument," accessed July 25, 2017, https://www.merriam-webster.com/dictionary/argument.
6. Gary R. Habermas and Michael R. Licona, *The Case for the Resurrection of Jesus* (Grand Rapids, MI: Kregel, 2004), 259n24; Michael R. Licona, *The Resurrection of Jesus: A New Historiographical Approach* (Downers Grove, IL: InterVarsity, 2010), 260n25.
7. Ibid.

Week 2

1. Richard Dawkins, "A Challenge to Atheists," *Free Enquiry* 22, no. 3 (2002).
2. Martin Schönfeld and Michael Thompson, "Kant's Philosophical Development," *Stanford Encyclopedia of Philosophy*, November 24, 2014, https://plato.stanford.edu/entries/kant-development/.
3. Michael Ruse, *Darwinism Defended: A Guide to the Evolution Controversies* (Reading, MA: Addison-Wesley, 1982), 322, as quoted in John C. Lennox, *God's Undertaker: Has Science Buried God?* (Oxford: Lion Books, 2009), 32.
4. Lennox, *God's Undertaker*, 38.
5. Ibid., 21.
6. Morris Kline, *Mathematics: The Loss of Certainty* (New York: Oxford University Press, 1980), 31, as quoted in Lennox, *God's Undertaker*, 21.
7. John C. Lennox, *Seven Days That Divide the World: The Beginning According to Genesis and Science* (Grand Rapids, MI: Zondervan, 2011), 150.
8. Robert Jastrow, *God and the Astronomers* (New York: W. W. Norton, 1978), 116.
9. Paul Davies, *The Mind of God* (London: Simon and Schuster, 1992), 81, as quoted in John C. Lennox, *God's Undertaker: Has Science Buried God?* (Oxford: Lion Books, 2009), 62.
10. Albert Einstein, "Physics and Reality" (1936), reprinted in *Ideas and Opinions*, trans. Sonja Bargmann (New York: Bonanza, 1954), 292.
11. C. S. Lewis, *Mere Christianity* (New York: HarperCollins, 2001), 38.
12. "Declaration of Independence: A Transcription," *National Archives*, accessed November 6, 2017, https://www.archives.gov/founding-docs/declaration-transcript.
13. Universal Declaration of Human Rights, December 10, 1948, article 1, http:// www.ohchr.org/EN/UDHR/Documents/UDHR_Translations/eng.pdf.
14. Lennox, *God's Undertaker*, 40.
15. Francis J. Beckwith and Gregory Koukl, *Relativism: Feet Firmly Planted in Midair* (Grand Rapids, MI: Baker, 1998), 168.

Week 3

1. Ravi Zacharias, "Think Again—Deep Questions," *Just Thinking,* August 28, 2014, http://rzim.org/just-thinking/think-again-deep-questions/.
2. Abdu H. Murray, *Grand Central Question: Answering the Critical Concerns of the Major Worldviews* (Downers Grove, IL: InterVarsity, 2013), 112.
3. Clay Jones, *Why Does God Allow Evil?* (Eugene, OR: Harvest House, 2017), 80.
4. Andy Stanley, *How Good Is Good Enough?* (Sisters, OR: Multnomah Publishers, 2003), 90.
5. Augustine, *Confessions* 1:1.
6. William G. T. Shedd, *Dogmatic Theology*, 3rd ed., ed. Alan W. Gomes (Phillipsburg, NJ: Presbyterian and Reformed Publishing Company, 2003), 222.

Week 4

1. Friedrich Nietzsche, *Thus Spoke Zarathustra: A Book for All and None* (Cambridge: Cambridge University Press, 2006), 75.
2. C. S. Lewis, *Mere Christianity* (New York: HarperCollins, 2001), 56.
3. American Humanist Association, Humanist Manifesto III (2003), accessed August 8, 2017, https://americanhumanist.org/what-is-humanism/manifesto3/.
4. Ibid.
5. Ibid.
6. Ibid.
7. Richard Dawkins, *River Out of Eden: A Darwinian View of Life* (New York: HarperCollins, 1995), 132–33, as quoted in Abdu H. Murray, *Grand Central Question: Answering the Critical Concerns of the Major Worldviews* (Downers Grove, IL: InterVarsity, 2013), 70.
8. Joel Marks, "An Amoral Manifesto I," *Philosophy Now 80* (August/September 2010): 30, as quoted in Murray, Grand Central Question, 76.
9. David Bentley Hart, *Atheist Delusions: The Christian Revolution and Its Fashionable Enemies* (New Haven, CT: Yale University Press, 2009), 167–68, as quoted in Murray, *Grand Central Question*, 113.
10. Dred Scott v. Sandford, 60 U.S. (19 How.) 393, 405 (1856) ("[Slaves] had no rights or privileges but such as those who held the power and the Government might choose to grant them.").
11. Os Guinness, *A Free People's Suicide: Sustainable Freedom and the American Future* (Downers Grove, IL: InterVarsity, 2012), 148.
12. American Humanist Association, Humanist Manifesto III.
13. Clay Jones, *Why Does God Allow Evil?* (Eugene, OR: Harvest House, 2017), 206.
14. Dallas Willard, *The Divine Conspiracy* (San Francisco: HarperCollins, 1998), 397, as quoted in Jones, *Why Does God Allow Evil?*, 205.

Week 5

1. Robert Nozick, *Anarchy, State, and Utopia* (New York: Basic Books, 1974), 42–45.
2. George Bernard Shaw, *A Treatise on Parents and Children* (Fairfield, IA: 1st World Library, 2004), 63, as quoted in Jones, *Why Does God Allow Evil?* 161.
3. Jack Nicholson, interview by Dotson Rader, *Parade Magazine*, December 12, 2007, http://ablogawayfromhome.blogspot.com/2007/12/interview-with-jack-nicholson-parade.html.
4. Mark Twain's letter to his wife, Olivia Clemens, July 17, 1889, as quoted in Jones, *Why Does God Allow Evil?* 100–101.
5. C. S. Lewis, *The Screwtape Letters* (New York: HarperCollins, 2001), 44.
6. Ravi Zacharias, Twitter post, February 11, 2014, 5:12 p.m., https://twitter.com/ravizacharias/status/433408300076380160?lang=en.
7. Os Guinness, *A Free People's Suicide: Sustainable Freedom and the American Future* (Downers Grove, IL: InterVarsity, 2012), 151–52.
8. C. S. Lewis, *The Problem of Pain* (New York: Macmillan, 1953), 132, as quoted in Clay Jones, *Why Does God Allow Evil?* (Eugene, OR: Harvest House, 2017), 160.
9. Westminster Shorter Catechism, Q&A #1, accessed August 17, 2017, http://www.reformed.org/documents/wsc/index.html?_top=http://www.reformed.org/documents/WSC.html.
10. Richard Swinburne, "A Theodicy of Heaven and Hell," *The Existence and Nature of God*, ed. Alfred J. Freddoso (Notre Dame: University of Notre Dame, 1983), 41, as quoted in Jones, *Why Does God Allow Evil?* 176.

Week 6

1. Jim Petersen and Michael Shamy, *The Insider: Bringing the Kingdom of God into Your Everyday World* (Tyndale House, 2003).
2. Portions of this content are adapted from the precourse materials of an evangelism track offered at the InterVarsity Christian Fellowship "Compelling" conference held in East Lansing, Michigan, in 2015.
3. D. A. Carson, *The Gospel According to John* (Grand Rapids, MI: Eerdmans, 1991), 215–16.
4. Ibid., 216–18.
5. Don Everts and Doug Schaupp, *I Once Was Lost: What Postmodern Skeptics Taught Us about Their Path to Jesus* (Downers Grove, IL: InterVarsity, 2008).

NOTES